DOVER · THRIFT · EDITIONS

Blake's Selected Poems

WILLIAM BLAKE

Selected by

David and Virginia Erdman

DOVER PUBLICATIONS, INC.
New York

DOVER THRIFT EDITIONS

GENERAL EDITOR: STANLEY APPELBAUM
EDITOR OF THIS VOLUME: THOMAS CROFTS

Copyright

Bibliographical Note

This Dover edition, first published in 1995, is a new selection by David and Virginia Erdman from *The Complete Poetry and Prose of William Blake*, edited by David Erdman, University of California Press, Berkeley and Los Angeles, 1965. The introductory Note, table of contents and index of titles and first lines have been prepared specially for the present edition.

Library of Congress Cataloging-in-Publication Data

Blake, William, 1757–1827.
   [Poems. Selections]
   Blake's selected poems / edited by David and Virginia Erdman.
      p.   cm. — (Dover thrift editions)
   Includes index.
   ISBN 0-486-28517-0 (pbk.)
   I. Erdman, David V.   II. Erdman, Virginia.   III. Title.   IV. Series.
PR4142.E7   1995
821'.7 — dc20   95-43180
                                                    CIP

Manufactured in the United States of America
Dover Publications, Inc., 31 East 2nd Street, Mineola, N.Y. 11501

Note

THE EARLY YOUTH OF THE POET, painter and engraver William Blake (1757–1827) was peaceful enough to allow him a comfortable, dreamy childhood and an unmolested beginning as an artist. His father, James Blake, a prosperous London haberdasher, encouraged his son's creative tendencies, sending him first to Pars's Drawing School, and later to the Royal Academy of Arts. Training as an artist and engraver, and reading Shakespeare, the King James Bible and Milton, the young Blake thought of England as a hale and happy Albion that bred beautiful poets and fostered beatific visions. During his apprentice days, however, the turbulence of the times began to make itself felt. The reign of George III (1760–1820) was marked in general by stormy relations between monarch, parliament and people. The British economy was staggered by the expense of the Seven Years' War; and unrest in the American colonies served to divide public opinion and further destabilize royal authority. In 1766, when Blake was nine, royal troops fired into a crowd protesting the arrest of a popular parliamentarian and, in what was called the Massacre at St. George's Fields, killed seven citizens. This was followed by the official (though probably untrue) announcement that "His Majesty is highly pleased" by the action of his troops. In 1770 the Boston Massacre occurred, angering the multitudes of British subjects who felt solidarity with the rebelling colonists. And in 1780 the Gordon Riots occurred, in which, for seven days, Londoners protesting George's policies in the New World broke open jails, freed prisoners and burned buildings; Blake was then 22 and in the crowd (though it is not thought that he had any hand in the destruction of property).

Coming of age in this London, Blake had found social and intellectual company among fellow artisans, painters and writers, and with them was electrified by the upheavals of the period, responding with them to the problems arising from industrial expansion, revolutions in America and France, and in general what were considered to be the evils of imperialism. The effect of these events upon Blake's painting and poetry are well known. It took him from the carefree poems and songs of his youth ("How sweet I roam'd from field to field") to the high rhetoric of prophecy ("The shadowy daughter of Urthona stood . . ."). But Blake had more modes than just these two.

This selection of the poems attempts to follow the lyrical impulse of the poet through the various phases of his writing. It includes the shorter pieces written during his youthful, non-prophetic phase; a large group of the political and satirical verses; epigrams; and lyric pieces from the prophecies. While some of these poems are to be found within the major poems and collections (*Marriage of Heaven and Hell*, *Songs of Innocence and Experience*), many are of scattered origins and stray through Blake's *oeuvre* unattached to the longer, more fully developed projects. These come from notebooks, odd manuscripts and prose works (*Jerusalem*, *An Island in the Moon*) which are interspersed with songs and poems. As well, there are many philosophical explorations and humorous divagations which, wonderful as they are, are often neglected in favor of Blake's more polished work. This book is an inclusive, well-rounded survey of the poet who, though thought of as a visionary and a prophet, also enjoyed scatological humor, urbane couplets and self-mockery. Like most great artists, Blake defies all efforts at crude categorizing.

Mr. and Mrs. Erdman have brought together a valuable collection of Blake's work which may serve as an index of the poet's preoccupations from youth to middle age; an introduction to his total body of work; and a testament to the ecstatic range of Blake's lyric gift.

Blake's own idiosyncratic spelling, punctuation and capitalization have been preserved.

Contents

v

Blake's
Selected Poems

To Spring

O thou, with dewy locks, who lookest down
Thro' the clear windows of the morning; turn
Thine angel eyes upon our western isle,
Which in full choir hails thy approach, O Spring!

The hills tell each other, and the list'ning
Vallies hear; all our longing eyes are turned
Up to thy bright pavillions: issue forth,
And let thy holy feet visit our clime.

Come o'er the eastern hills, and let our winds
Kiss thy perfumed garments; let us taste
Thy morn and evening breath; scatter thy pearls
Upon our love-sick land that mourns for thee.

O deck her forth with thy fair fingers; pour
Thy soft kisses on her bosom; and put
Thy golden crown upon her languish'd head,
Whose modest tresses were bound up for thee!

To Summer

O thou, who passest thro' our vallies in
Thy strength, curb thy fierce steeds, allay the heat
That flames from their large nostrils! thou, O Summer,
Oft pitched'st here thy golden tent, and oft
Beneath our oaks hast slept, while we beheld
With joy, thy ruddy limbs and flourishing hair.

Beneath our thickest shades we oft have heard
Thy voice, when noon upon his fervid car
Rode o'er the deep of heaven; beside our springs
Sit down, and in our mossy vallies, on
Some bank beside a river clear, throw thy
Silk draperies off, and rush into the stream:
Our vallies love the Summer in his pride.

Our bards are fam'd who strike the silver wire:
Our youth are bolder than the southern swains:

[handwritten: England is better than other lands]

[handwritten: England]

Our maidens fairer in the sprightly dance:
We lack not songs, nor instruments of joy,
Nor echoes sweet, nor waters clear as heaven,
Nor laurel wreaths against the sultry heat.

To Autumn

[handwritten: Joy w/ wine]
[handwritten: Music]

O Autumn, laden with fruit, and stained
With the blood of the grape, pass not, but sit
Beneath my shady roof, there thou may'st rest,
And tune thy jolly voice to my fresh pipe;
And all the daughters of the year shall dance!
Sing now the lusty song of fruits and flowers.

"The narrow bud opens her beauties to
"The sun, and love runs in her thrilling veins;
"Blossoms hang round the brows of morning, and
"Flourish down the bright cheek of modest eve,
"Till clust'ring Summer breaks forth into singing,
"And feather'd clouds strew flowers round her head.

[handwritten: Beauty]
[handwritten: Bounty]

"The spirits of the air live on the smells
"Of fruit; and joy, with pinions light, roves round
"The gardens, or sits singing in the trees."
Thus sang the jolly Autumn as he sat,
Then rose, girded himself, and o'er the bleak
Hills fled from our sight; but left his golden load.

To Winter

O Winter! bar thine adamantine doors:
The north is thine; there hast thou built thy dark
Deep-founded habitation. Shake not thy roofs,
Nor bend thy pillars with thine iron car.

[handwritten: like a heavy chariot]

He hears me not, but o'er the yawning deep
Rides heavy; his storms are unchain'd; sheathed
In ribbed steel, I dare not lift mine eyes;
For he hath rear'd his sceptre o'er the world.

[handwritten: a monster]

Lo! now the direful monster, whose skin clings
To his strong bones, strides o'er the groaning rocks:
He withers all in silence, and his hand
Unclothes the earth, and freezes up frail life.

He takes his seat upon the cliffs, the mariner
Cries in vain. Poor little wretch! that deal'st
With storms; till heaven smiles, and the monster
Is driv'n yelling to his caves beneath mount Hecla.

To the Evening Star

Thou fair-hair'd angel of the evening,
Now, while the sun rests on the mountains, light
Thy bright torch of love; thy radiant crown
Put on, and smile upon our evening bed!
Smile on our loves; and, while thou drawest the
Blue curtains of the sky, scatter thy silver dew
On every flower that shuts its sweet eyes
In timely sleep. Let thy west wind sleep on
The lake; speak si[l]ence with thy glimmering eyes,
And wash the dusk with silver. Soon, full soon,
Dost thou withdraw; then the wolf rages wide,
And the lion glares thro' the dun forest:
The fleeces of our flocks are cover'd with
Thy sacred dew: protect them with thine influence.

beauty, calm —

But the wolf and lion come when it goes

To Morning

O holy virgin! clad in purest white,
Unlock heav'n's golden gates, and issue forth;
Awake the dawn that sleeps in heaven; let light
Rise from the chambers of the east, and bring
The honied dew that cometh on waking day.
O radiant morning, salute the sun,
Rouz'd like a huntsman to the chace; and, with
Thy buskin'd feet, appear upon our hills.

Beautiful

Fair Elenor

The bell struck one, and shook the silent tower;
The graves give up their dead: fair Elenor
Walk'd by the castle gate, and looked in.
A hollow groan ran thro' the dreary vaults.

She shriek'd aloud, and sunk upon the steps
On the cold stone her pale cheek. Sickly smells

Wow! Like a Medieval Ballad

Of death, issue as from a sepulchre,
And all is silent but the sighing vaults.

Chill death withdraws his hand, and she revives;
Amaz'd, she finds herself upon her feet,
And, like a ghost, thro' narrow passages
Walking, feeling the cold walls with her hands.

Fancy returns, and now she thinks of bones,
And grinning skulls, and corruptible death,
Wrap'd in his shroud; and now, fancies she hears
Deep sighs, and sees pale sickly ghosts gliding.

At length, no fancy, but reality
Distracts her. A rushing sound, and the feet
Of one that fled, approaches — Ellen stood,
Like a dumb statue, froze to stone with fear.

The wretch approaches, crying, "The deed is done;
"Take this, and send it by whom thou wilt send;
"It is my life — send it to Elenor: —
"He's dead, and howling after me for blood!

"Take this," he cry'd; and thrust into her arms
A wet napkin, wrap'd about; then rush'd
Past, howling: she receiv'd into her arms
Pale death, and follow'd on the wings of fear.

They pass'd swift thro' the outer gate; the wretch,
Howling, leap'd o'er the wall into the moat,
Stifling in mud. Fair Ellen pass'd the bridge,
And heard a gloomy voice cry, "Is it done?"

As the deer wounded Ellen flew over
The pathless plain; as the arrows that fly
By night; destruction flies, and strikes in darkness,
She fled from fear, till at her house arriv'd.

Her maids await her; on her bed she falls,
That bed of joy, where erst her lord hath press'd:
"Ah, woman's fear!" she cry'd; "Ah, cursed duke!
"Ah, my dear lord! ah, wretched Elenor!

"My lord was like a flower upon the brows
"Of lusty May! Ah, life as frail as flower!
"O ghastly death! withdraw thy cruel hand,
"Seek'st thou that flow'r to deck thy horrid temples?

"My lord was like a star, in highest heav'n
"Drawn down to earth by spells and wickedness:
"My lord was like the opening eyes of day,
"When western winds creep softly o'er the flowers:

"But he is darken'd; like the summer's noon,
"Clouded; fall'n like the stately tree, cut down;
"The breath of heaven dwelt among his leaves.
"O Elenor, weak woman, fill'd with woe!"

Thus having spoke, she raised up her head,
And saw the bloody napkin by her side,
Which in her arms she brought; and now, tenfold
More terrified, saw it unfold itself.

Her eyes were fix'd; the bloody cloth unfolds,
Disclosing to her sight the murder'd head
Of her dear lord, all ghastly pale, clotted
With gory blood; it groan'd, and thus it spake:

"O Elenor, behold thy husband's head,
"Who, sleeping on the stones of yonder tower,
"Was 'reft of life by the accursed duke!
"A hired villain turn'd my sleep to death!

"O Elenor, beware the cursed duke,
"O give not him thy hand, now I am dead;
"He seeks thy love; who, coward, in the night,
"Hired a villain to bereave my life."

She sat with dead cold limbs, stiffen'd to stone;
She took the gory head up in her arms;
She kiss'd the pale lips; she had no tears to shed;
She hugg'd it to her breast, and groan'd her last.

Song

How sweet I roam'd from field to field,
    And tasted all the summer's pride,
'Till I the prince of love beheld,
    Who in the sunny beams did glide!

He shew'd me lilies for my hair,
    And blushing roses for my brow;
He led me through his gardens fair,
    Where all his golden pleasures grow.

With sweet May dews my wings were wet,
   And Phoebus fir'd my vocal rage;
He caught me in his silken net,
   And shut me in his golden cage.

He loves to sit and hear me sing,
   Then, laughing, sports and plays with me;
Then stretches out my golden wing,
   And mocks my loss of liberty.

Song

My silks and fine array,
   My smiles and languish'd air,
By love are driv'n away;
   And mournful lean Despair
Brings me yew to deck my grave:
Such end true lovers have.

His face is fair as heav'n,
   When springing buds unfold;
O why to him was't giv'n,
   Whose heart is wintry cold?
His breast is love's all worship'd tomb,
Where all love's pilgrims come.

Bring me an axe and spade,
   Bring me a winding sheet;
When I my grave have made,
   Let winds and tempests beat:
Then down I'll lie, as cold as clay.
True love doth pass away!

Song

Love and harmony combine,
And around our souls intwine,
While thy branches mix with mine,
And our roots together join.

Joys upon our branches sit,
Chirping loud, and singing sweet;

Like gentle streams beneath our feet
Innocence and virtue meet.

Thou the golden fruit dost bear,
I am clad in flowers fair;
Thy sweet boughs perfume the air,
And the turtle buildeth there.

There she sits and feeds her young,
Sweet I hear her mournful song;
And thy lovely leaves among,
There is love: I hear his tongue.

There his charming nest doth lay,
There he sleeps the night away;
There he sports along the day,
And doth among our branches play.

Song

I love the jocund dance,
    The softly-breathing song,
Where innocent eyes do glance,
    And where lisps the maiden's tongue.

I love the laughing vale,
    I love the echoing hill,
Where mirth does never fail,
    And the jolly swain laughs his fill.

I love the pleasant cot,
    I love the innocent bow'r.
Where white and brown is our lot,
    Or fruit in the mid-day hour.

I love the oaken seat,
    Beneath the oaken tree,
Where all the old villagers meet,
    And laugh our sports to see.

I love our neighbours all,
    But, Kitty, I better love thee;
And love them I ever shall;
    But thou art all to me.

Song

Memory, hither come,
   And tune your merry notes;
And, while upon the wind,
   Your music floats,
I'll pore upon the stream,
Where sighing lovers dream,
And fish for fancies as they pass
Within the watery glass.

I'll drink of the clear stream,
   And hear the linnet's song;
And there I'll lie and dream
   The day along:
And, when night comes, I'll go
   To places fit for woe;
Walking along the darken'd valley,
   With silent Melancholy.

Mad Song

The wild winds weep,
   And the night is a-cold;
Come hither, Sleep,
   And my griefs infold:
But lo! the morning peeps
   Over the eastern steeps,
And the rustling birds of dawn
The earth do scorn.

Lo! to the vault
   Of paved heaven,
With sorrow fraught
   My notes are driven:
They strike the ear of night,
   Make weep the eyes of day;
They make mad the roaring winds,
   And with tempests play.

Like a fiend in a cloud
   With howling woe,

After night I do croud,
   And with night will go;
I turn my back to the east,
From whence comforts have increas'd;
For light doth seize my brain
With frantic pain.

Song

Fresh from the dewy hill, the merry year
Smiles on my head, and mounts his flaming car;
Round my young brows the laurel wreathes a shade,
And rising glories beam around my head.

My feet are wing'd, while o'er the dewy lawn,
I meet my maiden, risen like the morn:
Oh bless those holy feet, like angels' feet;
Oh bless those limbs, beaming with heav'nly light!

Like as an angel glitt'ring in the sky,
In times of innocence, and holy joy;
The joyful shepherd stops his grateful song,
To hear the music of an angel's tongue.

So when she speaks, the voice of Heaven I hear
So when we walk, nothing impure comes near;
Each field seems Eden, and each calm retreat;
Each village seems the haunt of holy feet.

But that sweet village where my black-ey'd maid,
Closes her eyes in sleep beneath night's shade:
Whene'er I enter, more than mortal fire
Burns in my soul, and does my song inspire.

Song

When early morn walks forth in sober grey;
Then to my black ey'd maid I haste away,
When evening sits beneath her dusky bow'r,
And gently sighs away the silent hour;
The village bell alarms, away I go;
And the vale darkens at my pensive woe.

To that sweet village, where my black ey'd maid
Doth drop a tear beneath the silent shade,
I turn my eyes; and, pensive as I go,
Curse my black stars, and bless my pleasing woe.

Oft when the summer sleeps among the trees,
Whisp'ring faint murmurs to the scanty breeze,
I walk the village round; if at her side
A youth doth walk in stolen joy and pride,
I curse my stars in bitter grief and woe,
That made my love so high, and me so low.

O should she e'er prove false, his limbs I'd tear,
And throw all pity on the burning air;
I'd curse bright fortune for my mixed lot,
And then I'd die in peace, and be forgot.

To the Muses

Whether on Ida's shady brow,
    Or in the chambers of the East,
The chambers of the sun, that now
    From antient melody have ceas'd;

Whether in Heav'n ye wander fair,
    Or the green corners of the earth,
Or the blue regions of the air,
    Where the melodious winds have birth;

Whether on chrystal rocks ye rove,
    Beneath the bosom of the sea
Wand'ring in many a coral grove,
    Fair Nine, forsaking Poetry!

How have you left the antient love
    That bards of old enjoy'd in you!
The languid strings do scarcely move!
    The sound is forc'd, the notes are few!

Gwin, King of Norway

Come, Kings, and listen to my song,
   When Gwin, the son of Nore,
Over the nations of the North
   His cruel sceptre bore:

The Nobles of the land did feed
   Upon the hungry Poor;
They tear the poor man's lamb, and drive
   The needy from their door!

The land is desolate; our wives
   And children cry for bread;
Arise, and pull the tyrant down;
   Let Gwin be humbled.

Gordred the giant rous'd himself
   From sleeping in his cave;
He shook the hills, and in the clouds
   The troubl'd banners wave.

Beneath them roll'd, like tempests black,
   The num'rous sons of blood;
Like lions' whelps, roaring abroad,
   Seeking their nightly food.

Down Bleron's hills they dreadful rush,
   Their cry ascends the clouds;
The trampling horse, and clanging arms
   Like rushing mighty floods!

Their wives and children, weeping loud,
   Follow in wild array,
Howling like ghosts, furious as wolves
   In the bleak wintry day.

"Pull down the tyrant to the dust,
   "Let Gwin be humbled,"
They cry; "and let ten thousand lives
   "Pay for the tyrant's head."

From tow'r to tow'r the watchmen cry,
   "O Gwin, the son of Nore,
"Arouse thyself! the nations black,
   "Like clouds, come rolling o'er!"

Gwin rear'd his shield, his palace shakes,
   His chiefs come rushing round;
Each, like an awful thunder cloud,
   With voice of solemn sound.

Like reared stones around a grave
   They stand around the King;
Then suddenly each seiz'd his spear,
   And clashing steel does ring.

The husbandman does leave his plow,
   To wade thro' fields of gore;
The merchant binds his brows in steel,
   And leaves the trading shore:

The shepherd leaves his mellow pipe,
   And sounds the trumpet shrill;
The workman throws his hammer down
   To heave the bloody bill.

Like the tall ghost of Barraton,
   Who sports in stormy sky,
Gwin leads his host as black as night,
   When pestilence does fly.

With horses and with chariots —
   And all his spearmen bold,
March to the sound of mournful song,
   Like clouds around him roll'd.

Gwin lifts his hand — the nations halt;
   "Prepare for war," he cries —
Gordred appears! — his frowning brow
   Troubles our northern skies.

The armies stand, like balances
   Held in th' Almighty's hand; —
"Gwin, thou hast fill'd thy measure up,
   "Thou'rt swept from out the land."

And now the raging armies rush'd,
   Like warring mighty seas;
The Heav'ns are shook with roaring war,
   The dust ascends the skies!

Earth smokes with blood, and groans, and shakes,
   To drink her childrens' gore,

A sea of blood; nor can the eye
　　See to the trembling shore!

And on the verge of this wild sea
　　Famine and death doth cry;
The cries of women and of babes.
　　Over the field doth fly.

The King is seen raging afar;
　　With all his men of might;
Like blazing comets, scattering death
　　Thro' the red fev'rous night.

Beneath his arm like sheep they die,
　　And groan upon the plain;
The battle faints, and bloody men
　　Fight upon hills of slain.

Now death is sick, and riven men
　　Labour and toil for life;
Steed rolls on steed, and shield on shield,
　　Sunk in this sea of strife!

The god of war is drunk with blood,
　　The earth doth faint and fail;
The stench of blood makes sick the heav'ns;
　　Ghosts glut the throat of hell!

O what have Kings to answer for,
　　Before that awful throne!
When thousand deaths for vengeance cry,
　　And ghosts accusing groan!

Like blazing comets in the sky,
　　That shake the stars of light,
Which drop like fruit unto the earth,
　　Thro' the fierce burning night;

Like these did Gwin and Gordred meet,
　　And the first blow decides;
Down from the brow unto the breast
　　Gordred his head divides!

Gwin fell; the Sons of Norway fled,
　　All that remain'd alive;
The rest did fill the vale of death,
　　For them the eagles strive.

The river Dorman roll'd their blood
    Into the northern sea;
Who mourn'd his sons, and overwhelm'd
    The pleasant south country.

An Imitation of Spenser*

Golden Apollo, that thro' heaven wide
    Scatter'st the rays of light, and truth's beams!
In lucent words my darkling verses dight,
    And wash my earthy mind in thy clear streams,
    That wisdom may descend in fairy dreams:
All while the jocund hours in thy train
Scatter their fancies at thy poet's feet;
    And when thou yields to night thy wide domain,
Let rays of truth enlight his sleeping brain.

For brutish Pan in vain might thee assay
    With tinkling sounds to dash thy nervous verse,
Sound without sense; yet in his rude affray,
    (For ignorance is Folly's leesing nurse,
    And love of Folly needs none other curse;)
Midas the praise hath gain'd of lengthen'd eares,
    For which himself might deem him ne'er the worse
    To sit in council with his modern peers,
And judge of tinkling rhimes, and elegances terse.

And thou, Mercurius, that with winged brow
    Dost mount aloft into the yielding sky,
And thro' Heav'n's halls thy airy flight dost throw,
Entering with holy feet to where on high
Jove weighs the counsel of futurity;
    Then, laden with eternal fate, dost go
Down, like a falling star, from autumn sky,
And o'er the surface of the silent deep dost fly.

    If thou arrivest at the sandy shore,
Where nought but envious hissing adders dwell,
    Thy golden rod, thrown on the dusty floor,
Can charm to harmony with potent spell;

---

* Printed by Blake "Spencer" and left uncorrected.

Such is sweet Eloquence, that does dispel
   Envy and Hate, that thirst for human gore:
And cause in sweet society to dwell
Vile savage minds that lurk in lonely cell.

   O Mercury, assist my lab'ring sense,
That round the circle of the world wou'd fly!
   As the wing'd eagle scorns the tow'ry fence
Of Alpine hills round his high aery,
And searches thro' the corners of the sky,
   Sports in the clouds to hear the thunder's sound,
And see the winged lightnings as they fly,
   Then, bosom'd in an amber cloud, around
Plumes his wide wings, and seeks Sol's palace high.

   And thou, O warrior maid, invincible,
Arm'd with the terrors of Almighty Jove!
   Pallas, Minerva, maiden terrible,
Lov'st thou to walk the peaceful solemn grove,
   In solemn gloom of branches interwove?
Or bear'st thy Egis o'er the burning field,
   Where, like the sea, the waves of battle move?
Or have thy soft piteous eyes beheld
   The weary wanderer thro' the desert rove?
Or does th' afflicted man thy heav'nly bosom move?

Blind-man's Buff

When silver Snow decks Susan's cloaths,
And jewel hangs at th' shepherd's nose,
The blushing bank is all my care,
With hearth so red, and walls so fair;
"Heap the sea-coal; come, heap it higher,
"The oaken log lay on the fire:"
The well-wash'd stools, a circling row,
With lad and lass, how fair the show!
The merry can of nut-brown ale,
The laughing jest, the love-sick tale,
'Till tir'd of chat, the game begins,
The lasses prick the lads with pins;
Roger from Dolly twitch'd the stool,
She falling, kiss'd the ground, poor fool!

She blush'd so red, with side-long glance
At hob-nail Dick, who griev'd the chance.
But now for Blind-man's Buff they call;
Of each incumbrance clear the hall —
Jenny her silken kerchief folds,
And blear-ey'd Will the black lot holds;
Now laughing, stops, with "Silence! hush!"
And Peggy Pout gives Sam a push. ——
The Blind-man's arms, extended wide,
Sam slips between; — "O woe betide
Thee, clumsy Will!" — but titt'ring Kate
Is pen'd up in the corner strait!
And now Will's eyes beheld the play,
He thought his face was t'other way. ——
"Now, Kitty, now; what chance hast thou,
"Roger so near thee, Trips; I vow!["]
She catches him — then Roger ties
His own head up — but not his eyes;
For thro' the slender cloth he sees,
And runs at Sam, who slips with ease
His clumsy hold; and, dodging round,
Sukey is tumbled on the ground! ——
"See what it is to play unfair!
"Where cheating is, there's mischief there."
But Roger still pursues the chace, —
"He sees! he sees!["] cries softly Grace;
"O Roger, thou, unskill'd in art,
"Must, surer bound, go thro' thy part!"
Now Kitty, pert, repeats the rhymes,
And Roger turns him round three times;
Then pauses ere he starts —— but Dick
Was mischief bent upon a trick:
Down on his hands and knees he lay,
Directly in the Blind-man's way —
Then cries out, "Hem!" Hodge heard, and ran
With hood-wink'd chance — sure of his man;
But down he came. — Alas, how frail
Our best of hopes, how soon they fail!
With crimson drops he stains the ground,
Confusion startles all around!
Poor piteous Dick supports his head,
And fain would cure the hurt he made;
But Kitty hasted with a key,

And down his back they strait convey
The cold relief — the blood is stay'd,
And Hodge again holds up his head.
Such are the fortunes of the game,
And those who play should stop the same
By wholesome laws; such as[:] all those
Who on the blinded man impose,
Stand in his stead; as long a-gone
When men were first a nation grown;
Lawless they liv'd — till wantonness
And liberty began t' increase;
And one man lay in another's way,
Then laws were made to keep fair play.

Song 1st by a Shepherd

Welcome stranger to this place,
Where joy doth sit on every bough,
Paleness flies from every face,
We reap not, what we do not sow.

Innocence doth like a Rose,
Bloom on every Maidens cheek;
Honor twines around her brows,
The jewel Health adorns her neck.

Song 3ᵈ by an Old Shepherd

When silver snow decks Sylvio's clothes
And jewel hangs at shepherd's nose,
We can abide life's pelting storm
That makes our limbs quake, if our hearts be warm.

Whilst Virtue is our walking staff,
And Truth a lantern to our path;
We can abide life's pelting storm
That makes our limbs quake, if our hearts be warm.

Blow boisterous Wind, stern Winter frown,
Innocence is a Winter's gown;
So clad, we'll abide life's pelting storm
That makes our limbs quake, if our hearts be warm.

"Never pain to tell thy Love"

Never pain to tell thy Love
Love that never told can be
For the gentle wind does move
Silently invisibly

I told my love I told my love
I told her all my heart
Trembling cold in ghastly fears
Ah she doth depart

Soon as she was gone from me
A traveller came by
Silently invisibly
O was no deny

"I feard the fury of my wind"

I feard the fury of my wind
Would blight all blossoms fair & true
And my sun it shind & shind
And my wind it never blew

But a blossom fair or true
Was not found on any tree
For all blossoms grew & grew
Fruitless false tho fair to see

"I saw a chapel all of gold"

I saw a chapel all of gold
That none did dare to enter in
And many weeping stood without
Weeping mourning worshipping

I saw a serpent rise between
The white pillars of the door
And he forcd & forcd & forcd
Down the golden hinges tore

And along the pavement sweet
Set with pearls & rubies bright

All his slimy length he drew
Till upon the altar white

Vomiting his poison out
On the bread & on the wine
So I turnd into a sty
And laid me down among the swine

He sees a horrible serpent Blake is corrupt

"I laid me down upon a bank"

I laid me down upon a bank
Where love lay sleeping
I heard among the rushes dank
Weeping Weeping

Then I went to the heath & the wild
To the thistles & thorns of the waste·
And they told me how they were beguild
Driven out & compeld to be chaste

A Cradle Song

Sleep Sleep beauty bright
Dreaming oer the joys of night
Sleep Sleep: in thy sleep
Little sorrows sit & weep

Sweet Babe in thy face
Soft desires I can trace
Secret joys & secret smiles
Little pretty infant wiles

As thy softest limbs I feel
Smiles as of the morning steal
Oer thy cheek & oer thy breast
Where thy little heart does rest

O the cunning wiles that creep
In thy little heart asleep
When thy little heart does wake
Then the dreadful lightnings break

From thy cheek & from thy eye
Oer the youthful harvests nigh
Infant wiles & infant smiles
Heaven & Earth of peace beguiles

"I askéd a thief to steal me a peach"

I askéd a thief to steal me a peach
He turned up his eyes
I ask'd a lithe lady to lie her down
Holy & meek she cries —

As soon as I went
An angel came.
He wink'd at the thief
And smild at the dame —

And without one word said
Had a peach from the tree
And still as a maid
Enjoy'd the lady.

To My Mirtle

To a lovely mirtle bound
Blossoms showring all around
O how sick & weary I
Underneath my mirtle lie
Why should I be bound to thee
O my lovely mirtle tree

"O lapwing thou fliest around the heath"

O lapwing thou fliest around the heath
Nor seest the net that is spread beneath
Why dost thou not fly among the corn fields
They cannot spread nets where a harvest yields

An Answer to the Parson

Why of the sheep do you not learn peace ·
Because I dont want you to shear my fleece

[Experiment]*

Thou hast a lap full of seed
And this is a fine country
Why dost thou not cast thy seed
And live in it merrily

Shall I cast it on the sand
And turn it into fruitful land
For on no other ground
Can I sow my seed
Without tearing up
Some stinking weed

Riches

The countless gold of a merry heart
The rubies & pearls of a loving eye
The indolent never can bring to the mart
Nor the secret hoard up in his treasury

"If you trap the moment before its ripe"

If you trap the moment before its ripe
The tears of repentance youll certainly wipe
But if once you let the ripe moment go
You can never wipe off the tears of woe

"I heard an Angel singing"

I heard an Angel singing
When the day was springing
Mercy Pity Peace
Is the worlds release

Thus he sung all day
Over the new mown hay
Till the sun went down
And haycocks looked brown

---

* Title supplied by Professor Erdman.

I heard a Devil curse
Over the heath & the furze
Mercy could be no more
If there was nobody poor

And pity no more could be
If all were as happy as we
At his curse the sun went down
And the heavens gave a frown

Down pourd the heavy rain
Over the new reapd grain
And Miseries increase
Is Mercy Pity Peace

"Silent Silent Night"

Silent Silent Night
Quench the holy light
Of thy torches bright

For possessd of Day
Thousand spirits stray
That sweet joys betray

Why should joys be sweet
Used with deceit
Nor with sorrows meet

But an honest joy
Does itself destroy
For a harlot coy

To Nobodaddy

Why art thou silent & invisible
Father of Jealousy
Why dost thou hide thyself in clouds
From every searching Eye

Why darkness & obscurity
In all thy words & laws
That none dare eat the fruit but from

The wily serpents jaws
Or is it because Secresy
gains females loud applause

[How to know Love from Deceit]*

Love to faults is always blind
Always is to joy inclind
Lawless wingd & unconfind
And breaks all chains from every mind

Deceit to secresy confind
Lawful cautious & refind
To every thing but interest blind
And forges fetters for the mind

The Wild Flowers Song

As I wanderd the forest
The green leaves among
I heard a wild flower
Singing a Song

I slept in the earth
In the silent night
I murmurd my fears
And I felt delight

In the morning I went
As rosy as morn
To seek for new Joy
But I met with scorn

Soft Snow

I walked abroad in a snowy day
I askd the soft snow with me to play
She playd & she melted in all her prime
And the winter calld it a dreadful crime

---

* This title was added by the poet after composition and later deleted.

Merlins Prophecy

The harvest shall flourish in wintry weather
When two virginities meet together

The King & the Priest must be tied in a tether
Before two virgins can meet together

"Why should I care for the men of thames"

Why should I care for the men of thames
Or the cheating waves of charterd streams
Or shrink at the little blasts of fear
That the hireling blows into my ear

Tho born on the cheating banks of Thames
Tho his waters bathed my infant limbs
The Ohio shall wash his stains from me
I was born a slave but I go to be free

Day

The Sun arises in the East
Clothd in robes of blood & gold
Swords & spears & wrath increast
All around his bosom rolld
Crownd with warlike fires & raging desires

"The sword sung on the barren heath"

The sword sung on the barren heath
The sickle in the fruitful field
The sword he sung a song of death
But could not make the sickle yield

"Abstinence sows sand all over"

Abstinence sows sand all over
The ruddy limbs & flaming hair
But Desire Gratified
Plants fruits of life & beauty there

"In a wife I would desire"

In a wife I would desire
What in whores is always found
The lineaments of Gratified desire

Lacedemonian Instruction

Come hither my boy tell me what thou seest there
A fool tangled in a religious snare

"An old maid early eer I knew"

An old maid early eer I knew
Ought but the love that on me grew
And now Im coverd oer & oer
And wish that I had been a Whore

O I cannot cannot find
The undaunted courage of a Virgin Mind
For Early I in love was crost
Before my flower of love was lost

Several Questions Answerd

He who binds to himself a joy
Doth the winged life destroy
But he who kisses the joy as it flies
Lives in Eternitys sun rise

*

The look of love alarms
Because tis filld with fire
But the look of soft deceit
Shall Win the lovers hire

*

Soft deceit & Idleness
These are Beautys sweetest dress

*

What is it men in women do require
The lineaments of Gratified Desire
What is it women do in men require
The lineaments of Gratified Desire

An Ancient Proverb

Remove away that blackning church
Remove away that marriage hearse
Remove away that —— of blood
Youll quite remove the ancient curse

The Fairy

Come hither my sparrows
My little arrows
If a tear or a smile
Will a man beguile
If an amorous delay
Clouds a sunshiny day
If the step of a foot
Smites the heart to its root
Tis the marriage ring
Makes each fairy a king

So a fairy sung
From the leaves I sprung
He leapd from the spray
To flee away
But in my hat caught
He soon shall be taught
Let him laugh let him cry
Hes my butterfly
For I've pulld out the Sting
Of the marriage ring

"My Spectre around me night & day"

My Spectre around me night & day
Like a Wild beast guards my way
My Emanation far within
Weeps incessantly for my Sin

A Fathomless & boundless deep
There we wander there we weep
On the hungry craving wind
My Spectre follows thee behind

He scents thy footsteps in the snow
Wheresoever thou dost go
Thro the wintry hail & rain
When wilt thou return again

Dost thou not in Pride & scorn
Fill with tempests all my morn
And with jealousies & fears
Fill my pleasant nights with tears

Seven of my sweet loves thy knife
Has bereaved of their life
Their marble tombs I built with tears
And with cold & shuddering fears

Seven more loves weep night & day
Round the tombs where my loves lay
And seven more loves attend each night
Around my couch with torches bright

And seven more Loves in my bed
Crown with wine my mournful head
Pitying & forgiving all
Thy transgressions great & small

When wilt thou return & view
My loves & them to life renew
When wilt thou return & live
When wilt thou pity as I forgive

Never Never I return
Still for Victory I burn
Living thee alone Ill have
And when dead Ill be thy Grave

Thro the Heavn & Earth & Hell
Thou shalt never never quell
I will fly & thou pursue
Night & Morn the flight renew

Till I turn from Female Love
And root up the Infernal Grove
I shall never worthy be
To Step into Eternity

And to end thy cruel mocks
Annihilate thee on the rocks
And another form create
To be subservient to my Fate

Let us agree to give up Love
And root up the infernal grove
Then shall we return & see
The worlds of happy Eternity

& Throughout all Eternity
I forgive you you forgive me
As our dear Redeemer said
This the Wine & this the Bread

[Postscript]*

Oer my Sins Thou sit & moan
Hast thou no Sins of thy own
Oer my Sins thou sit & weep
And lull thy own Sins fast asleep

What Transgressions I commit
Are for thy Transgressions fit
They thy Harlots thou their Slave
And my Bed becomes their Grave

Poor pale pitiable form
That I follow in a Storm
Iron tears & groans of lead
Bind around my akeing head

---

* Title supplied by Professor Erdman.

And let us go to the highest downs
With many pleasing wiles
The Woman that does not love your Frowns
Will never embrace your smiles

"Mock on Mock on Voltaire Rousseau"

Mock on Mock on Voltaire Rousseau
Mock on Mock on! tis all in vain!
You throw the sand against the wind
And the wind blows it back again

And every sand becomes a Gem
Reflected in the beams divine
Blown back they blind the mocking Eye
But still in Israels paths they shine

The Atoms of Democritus
And Newtons Particles of light
Are sands upon the Red sea shore
Where Israels tents do shine so bright

Morning

To find the western path
Right thro the gates of Wrath
I urge my way
Sweet Mercy leads me on
With soft repentant moan
I see the break of day

The war of swords & spears
Melted by dewy tears
Exhales on high
The Sun is freed from fears
And with soft grateful tears
Ascends the sky

The Birds

He.   Where thou dwellest in what Grove
      Tell me Fair one tell me love
      Where thou thy charming Nest dost build
      O thou pride of every field

She.   Yonder stands a lonely tree
      There I live & mourn for thee
      Morning drinks my silent tear
      And evening winds my sorrows bear

He.   O thou Summers harmony
      I have livd & mournd for thee
      Each day I mourn along the wood
      And night hath heard my sorrows loud

She.   Dost thou truly long for me
      And am I thus sweet to thee
      Sorrow now is at an End
      O my Lover & my Friend

He.   Come on wings of joy well fly
      To where my Bower hangs on high
      Come & make thy calm retreat
      Among green leaves & blossoms sweet

"Why was Cupid a Boy"

Why was Cupid a Boy
And why a boy was he
He should have been a Girl
For ought that I can see

For he shoots with his bow
And the Girl shoots with her Eye
And they both are merry & glad
And laugh when we do cry

And to make Cupid a Boy
Was the Cupid Girls mocking plan
For a boy cant interpret the thing
Till he is become a man

And then hes so piercd with care
And wounded with arrowy smarts
That the whole business of his life
Is to pick out the heads of the darts

Twas the Greeks love of war
Turnd Love into a Boy
And Woman into a Statue of Stone
And away fled every Joy

To the Queen

The Door of Death is made of Gold,
That Mortal Eyes cannot behold;
But, when the Mortal Eyes are clos'd,
And cold and pale the Limbs repos'd,
The Soul awakes; and, wond'ring, sees
In her mild Hand the golden Keys:
The Grave is Heaven's golden Gate,
And rich and poor around it wait;
O Shepherdess of England's Fold,
Behold this Gate of Pearl and Gold!

To dedicate to England's Queen
The Visions that my Soul has seen,
And, by Her kind permission, bring
What I have borne on solemn Wing,
From the vast regions of the Grave,
Before Her Throne my Wings I wave;
Bowing before my Sov'reign's Feet,
"The Grave produc'd these Blossoms sweet
"In mild repose from Earthly strife;
"The Blossoms of Eternal Life!"

"The Caverns of the Grave Ive seen"

The Caverns of the Grave Ive seen
And these I shewd to Englands Queen
But now the Caves of Hell I view
Who shall I dare to shew them to
What mighty Soul in Beautys form
Shall dauntless View the Infernal Storm

Egremonts Countess can controll
The flames of Hell that round me roll
If she refuse I still go on
Till the Heavens & Earth are gone
Still admird by Noble minds
Followd by Envy on the winds
Reengravd Time after Time
Ever in their Youthful prime
My Designs unchangd remain
Time may rage but rage in vain
For above Times troubled Fountains
On the Great Atlantic Mountains
In my Golden House on high
There they Shine Eternally

"I rose up at the dawn of day"

I rose up at the dawn of day
Get thee away get thee away
Prayst thou for Riches away away
This is the Throne of Mammon grey

Said I this sure is very odd
I took it to be the Throne of God
For every Thing besides I have
It is only for Riches that I can crave

I have Mental Joy & Mental Health
And Mental Friends & Mental wealth
Ive a Wife I love & that loves me
Ive all But Riches Bodily

I am in Gods presence night & day
And he never turns his face away
The accuser of sins by my side does stand
And he holds my money bag in his hand

For my worldly things God makes him pay
And hed pay for more if to him I would pray
And so you may do the worst you can do
Be assurd Mr Devil I wont pray to you

Then If for Riches I must not Pray
God knows I little of Prayers need say

He finds he is led to pray to the Devil for money! but he wont do it. He has all else good that he needs.

So as a Church is known by its Steeple
If I pray it must be for other People

He says if I do not worship him for a God
I shall eat coarser food & go worse shod
So as I dont value such things as these
You must do Mr Devil just as God please

little money because it has not the great value.

"A fairy skipd upon my knee"   ?

A fairy skipd upon my knee
Singing & dancing merrily
I said Thou thing of patches rings
Pins Necklaces & such like things
Disguiser of the Female Form
Thou paltry gilded poisnous worm
Weeping he fell upon my thigh
And thus in tears did soft reply
Knowest thou not O Fairies Lord
How much by us Contemnd Abhorrd
Whatever hides the Female form
That cannot bear the Mental storm
Therefore in Pity still we give
Our lives to make the Female live
And what would turn into disease
We turn to what will joy & please

To Mrs Ann Flaxman

A little Flower grew in a lonely Vale
Its form was lovely but its colours. pale
One standing in the Porches of the Sun
When his Meridian Glories were begun
Leapd from the steps of fire & on the grass
Alighted where this little flower was
With hands divine he movd the gentle Sod
And took the Flower up in its native Clod
Then planting it upon a Mountains brow
'Tis your own fault if you dont flourish now

The Smile

There is a Smile of Love
And there is a Smile of Deceit
And there is a Smile of Smiles
In which these two Smiles meet

And there is a Frown of Hate
And there is a Frown of Disdain
And there is a Frown of Frowns
Which you strive to forget in vain

For it sticks in the Hearts deep Core
And it sticks in the deep Back bone
And no Smile that ever was smild
But only one Smile alone

That betwixt the Cradle & Grave
It only once Smild can be
But when it once is Smild
Theres an end to all Misery

The Golden Net

Three Virgins at the break of day
Whither young Man whither away
Alas for woe! alas for woe!
They cry & tears for ever flow
The one was Clothd in flames of fire
The other Clothd in iron wire
The other Clothd in tears & sighs
Dazling bright before my Eyes
They bore a Net of Golden twine
To hang upon the Branches fine
Pitying I wept to see the woe
That Love & Beauty undergo
To be consumd in burning Fires
And in ungratified Desires
And in tears clothd Night & day
Melted all my Soul away
When they saw my Tears a Smile
That did Heaven itself beguile
Bore the Golden Net aloft

As on downy Pinions soft
Over the Morning of my Day
Underneath the Net I stray
Now intreating Burning Fire
Now intreating Iron Wire
Now intreating Tears & Sighs
O when will the morning rise

The Mental Traveller

I traveld thro' a Land of Men
A Land of Men & Women too
And heard & saw such dreadful things
As cold Earth wanderers never knew

For there the Babe is born in joy
That was begotten in dire woe
Just as we Reap in joy the fruit
Which we in bitter tears did Sow

And if the Babe is born a Boy
He's given to a Woman Old
Who nails him down upon a rock
Catches his Shrieks in Cups of gold

She binds iron thorns around his head
She pierces both his hands & feet
She cuts his heart out at his side
To make it feel both cold & heat

Her fingers number every Nerve
Just as a Miser counts his gold
She lives upon his shrieks & cries
And She grows young as he grows old

Till he becomes a bleeding youth
And she becomes a Virgin bright
Then he rends up his Manacles
And binds her down for his delight

He plants himself in all her Nerves
Just as a Husbandman his mould
And She becomes his dwelling place
And Garden fruitful Seventy fold

An aged Shadow soon he fades
Wandring round an Earthly Cot
Full filled all with gems & gold
Which he by industry had got

And these are the gems of the Human Soul
The rubies & pearls of a lovesick eye
The countless gold of the akeing heart
The martyrs groan & the lovers sigh

They are his meat they are his drink
He feeds the Beggar & the Poor
And the way faring Traveller
For ever open is his door

His grief is their eternal joy
They make the roofs & walls to ring
Till from the fire on the hearth
A little Female Babe does spring

And she is all of solid fire
And gems & gold that none his hand
Dares stretch to touch her Baby form
Or wrap her in his swaddling-band

But She comes to the Man she loves
If young or old or rich or poor
They soon drive out the aged Host
A Begger at anothers door

He wanders weeping far away
Untill some other take him in
Oft blind & age-bent sore distrest
Untill he can a Maiden win

And to Allay his freezing Age
The Poor Man takes her in his arms
The Cottage fades before his Sight
The Garden & its lovely Charms

The Guests are scatterd thro' the land
For the Eye altering alters all
The Senses roll themselves in fear
And the flat Earth becomes a Ball

The Stars Sun Moon all shrink away
A desart vast without a bound

And nothing left to eat or drink
And a dark desart all around

The honey of her Infant lips
The bread & wine of her sweet smile
The wild game of her roving Eye
Does him to Infancy beguile

For as he eats & drinks he grows
Younger & younger every day
And on the desart wild they both
Wander in terror & dismay

Like the wild Stag she flees away
Her fear plants many a thicket wild
While he pursues her night & day
By various arts of Love beguild

By various arts of Love & Hate
Till the wide desart planted oer
With Labyrinths of wayward Love
Where roams the Lion Wolf & Boar

Till he becomes a wayward Babe
And she a weeping Woman Old
Then many a Lover wanders here
The Sun & Stars are nearer rolld

The trees bring forth sweet Extacy
To all who in the desart roam
Till many a City there is Built
And many a pleasant Shepherds home

But when they find the frowning Babe
Terror strikes thro the region wide
They cry the Babe the Babe is Born
And flee away on Every side

For who dare touch the frowning form
His arm is witherd to its root
Lions Boars Wolves all howling flee
And every Tree does shed its fruit

And none can touch that frowning form
Except it be a Woman Old
She nails him down upon the Rock
And all is done as I have told

The Land of Dreams

Awake awake my little Boy
Thou wast thy Mothers only joy
Why dost thou weep in thy gentle sleep
Awake thy Father does thee keep

O what Land is the Land of Dreams
What are its Mountains & what are its Streams
O Father I saw my Mother there
Among the Lillies by waters fair

Among the Lambs clothed in white
She walkd with her Thomas in sweet delight
I wept for joy like a dove I mourn
O when shall I again return

Dear Child I also by pleasant Streams
Have wanderd all Night in the Land of Dreams
But tho calm & warm the Waters wide
I could not get to the other side

Father O Father what do we here
In this Land of unbelief & fear
The Land of Dreams is better far
Above the light of the Morning Star

Mary

Sweet Mary the first time she ever was there
Came into the Ball room among the Fair
The young Men & Maidens around her throng
And these are the words upon every tongue

An Angel is here from the heavenly Climes
Or again does return the Golden times
Her eyes outshine every brilliant ray
She opens her lips tis the Month of May

Mary moves in soft beauty & conscious delight
To augment with sweet smiles all the joys of the Night
Nor once blushes to own to the rest of the Fair
That sweet Love & Beauty are worthy our care

[handwritten marginalia: After first Ball Marys admired for her beauty by all.]

In the Morning the Villagers rose with delight
And repeated with pleasure the joys of the night
And Mary arose among Friends to be free
But no Friend from henceforward thou Mary shalt see

Some said she was proud some calld her a whore
And some when she passed by shut to the door
A damp cold came oer her her blushes all fled
Her lillies & roses are blighted & shed

O why was I born with a different Face
Why was I not born like this Envious Race
Why did Heaven adorn me with bountiful hand
And then set me down in an envious Land

To be weak as a Lamb & smooth as a Dove
And not to raise Envy is calld Christian Love
But if you raise Envy your Merits to blame
For planting such spite in the weak & the tame

I will humble my Beauty I will not dress fine
I will keep from the Ball & my Eyes shall not shine
And if any Girls Lover forsakes her for me
I'll refuse him my hand & from Envy be free

She went out in Morning attird plain & neat
Proud Marys gone Mad said the Child in the Street
She went out in Morning in plain neat attire
And came home in Evening bespatterd with mire

She trembled & wept sitting on the Bed side
She forgot it was Night & she trembled & cried
She forgot it was Night she forgot it was Morn
Her soft Memory imprinted with Faces of Scorn

With Faces of Scorn & with Eyes of disdain
Like foul Fiends inhabiting Marys mild Brain
She remembers no Face like the Human Divine
All Faces have Envy sweet Mary but thine

And thine is a Face of sweet Love in Despair
And thine is a Face of mild sorrow & care
And thine is a Face of wild terror & fear
That shall never be quiet till laid on its bier

[Handwritten margin notes:] But Envy drives all to shun and slander her! she questions why she was made lovely & why others one envious. so she goes out dressed plainly, and vows not to even talk to any girls lover. she gets mad from the rejection — she remembers only the scorn.

The Crystal Cabinet

The Maiden caught me in the Wild
Where I was dancing merrily
She put me into her Cabinet
And Lockd me up with a golden Key

This Cabinet is formd of Gold
And Pearl & Crystal shining bright
And within it opens into a World
And a little lovely Moony Night

Another England there I saw
Another London with its Tower
Another Thames & other Hills
And another pleasant Surrey Bower

Another Maiden like herself
Translucent lovely shining clear
Threefold each in the other closd
O what a pleasant trembling fear

O what a smile a threefold Smile
Filld me that like a flame I burnd
I bent to Kiss the lovely Maid
And found a Threefold Kiss returnd

I strove to sieze the inmost Form
With ardor fierce & hands of flame
But burst the Crystal Cabinet
And like a Weeping Babe became

A weeping Babe upon the wild
And Weeping Woman pale reclind
And in the outward Air again
I filld with woes the passing Wind

The Grey Monk

I die I die the Mother said
My Children die for lack of Bread
What more has the merciless Tyrant said
The Monk sat down on the Stony Bed

The blood red ran from the Grey Monks side
His hands & feet were wounded wide
His Body bent his arms & knees
Like to the roots of ancient trees

His eye was dry no tear could flow
A hollow groan first spoke his woe
He trembled & shudderd upon the Bed
At length with a feeble cry he said

When God commanded this hand to write
In the studious hours of deep midnight
He told me the writing I wrote should prove
The Bane of all that on Earth I lovd

My Brother starvd between two Walls
His Childrens Cry my Soul appalls
I mockd at the wrack & griding chain
My bent body mocks their torturing pain

Thy Father drew his sword in the North
With his thousands strong he marched forth
Thy Brother has armd himself in Steel
To avenge the wrongs thy Children feel

But vain the Sword & vain the Bow
They never can work Wars overthrow
The Hermits Prayer & the Widows tear
Alone can free the World from fear

For a Tear is an Intellectual Thing
And a Sigh is the Sword of an Angel King
And the bitter groan of the Martyrs woe
Is an Arrow from the Almighties Bow

The hand of Vengeance found the Bed
To which the Purple Tyrant fled
The iron hand crushd the Tyrants head
And became a Tyrant in his stead

Auguries of Innocence

[AN EDITORIAL ARRANGEMENT]*

To see a World in a Grain of Sand
And a Heaven in a Wild Flower
Hold Infinity in the palm of your hand
And Eternity in an hour

A Robin Red breast in a Cage
Puts all Heaven in a Rage
A Dove house filld with Doves & Pigeons
Shudders Hell thro all its regions
A dog starvd at his Masters Gate
Predicts the ruin of the State
A Horse misusd upon the Road
Calls to Heaven for Human blood
Each outcry of the hunted Hare
A fibre from the Brain does tear
A Skylark wounded in the wing
A Cherubim does cease to sing
The Game Cock clipd & armd for fight
Does the Rising Sun affright
The Lamb misusd breeds Public Strife
And yet forgives the Butchers Knife
He who shall train the Horse to War
Shall never pass the Polar Bar
Every Wolfs & Lions howl
Raises from Hell a Human Soul
The Bleat the Bark Bellow & Roar
Are Waves that Beat on Heavens Shore
The wild deer wandring here & there

---

* Following the lead of John Sampson, who printed the text in ms order followed
by a "revised version for those who may prefer to read the poem as a whole,
instead of as a number of disconnected proverb-couplets," and assisted by the
specific suggestions of John Grant (in correspondence), I have presented a
thematically grouped rearrangement. I concede that Blake may have wished
each reader to cope with this "Riddle" by himself. The "editorial arrangement" is
not presented as in any sense an improvement upon the text but as a thematic
analysis of it.

Keeps the Human Soul from Care
The Beggers Dog & Widows Cat
Feed them & thou wilt grow fat
He who shall hurt the little Wren
Shall never be belovd by Men
He who the Ox to wrath has movd
Shall never be by Woman lovd
He who torments the Chafers sprite
Weaves a Bower in endless Night
The wanton Boy that kills the Fly
Shall feel the Spiders enmity
The Catterpiller on the Leaf
Repeats to thee thy Mothers grief
Kill not the Moth nor Butterfly
For the Last Judgment draweth nigh
The Bat that flits at close of Eve
Has left the Brain that wont Believe
The Owl that calls upon the Night
Speaks the Unbelievers fright
The Gnat that sings his Summers song
Poison gets from Slanders tongue
The poison of the Snake & Newt
Is the sweat of Envys Foot
The Poison of the Honey Bee
Is the Artists Jealousy
A Riddle or the Crickets Cry
Is to Doubt a fit Reply
The Emmets Inch & Eagles Mile
Make Lame Philosophy to smile
He who Doubts from what he sees
Will neer Believe do what you Please
If the Sun & Moon should Doubt
Theyd immediately Go out
He who mocks the Infants Faith
Shall be mock'd in Age & Death
He who shall teach the Child to Doubt
The rotting Grave shall neer get out
He who respects the Infants faith
Triumphs over Hell & Death
The Childs Toys & the Old Mans Reasons
Are the Fruits of the Two seasons
The Questioner who sits so sly

Shall never know how to Reply
He who replies to words of Doubt
Doth put the Light of Knowledge out
A Truth thats told with bad intent
Beats all the Lies you can invent
Joy & Woe are woven fine
A Clothing for the Soul divine
Under every grief & pine
Runs a joy with silken twine
It is right it should be so
Man was made for Joy & Woe
And when this we rightly know
Thro the World we safely go
The Babe is more than swadling Bands
Throughout all these Human Lands
Tools were made & Born were hands
Every Farmer Understands
Every Tear from Every Eye
Becomes a Babe in Eternity
This is caught by Females bright
And returnd to its own delight
The Babe that weeps the Rod beneath
Writes Revenge in realms of Death
The Princes Robes & Beggars Rags
Are Toadstools on the Misers Bags
The Beggars Rags fluttering in Air
Does to Rags the Heavens tear
The poor Mans Farthing is worth more
Than all the Gold on Africs Shore
One Mite wrung from the Labrers hands
Shall buy & sell the Misers Lands
Or if protected from on high
Does that whole Nation sell & buy
The Strongest Poison ever known
Came from Caesars Laurel Crown
Nought can Deform the Human Race
Like to the Armours iron brace
The Soldier armd with Sword & Gun
Palsied strikes the Summers Sun
When Gold & Gems adorn the Plow
To peaceful Arts shall Envy Bow
To be in a Passion you Good may Do

But no Good if a Passion is in you
The Whore & Gambler by the State
Licencd build that Nations Fate
The Harlots cry from Street to Street
Shall weave Old Englands winding Sheet
The Winners Shout the Losers Curse
Dance before dead Englands Hearse
Every Night & every Morn
Some to Misery are Born
Every Morn & every Night
Some are Born to sweet delight
Some are Born to sweet delight
Some are Born to Endless Night
We are led to Believe a Lie
When we see not Thro the Eye
Which was Born in a Night to perish in a Night
When the Soul Slept in Beams of Light
God Appears & God is Light
To those poor Souls who dwell in Night
But does a Human Form Display
To those who Dwell in Realms of day

William Bond

I wonder whether the Girls are mad
And I wonder whether they mean to kill
And I wonder if William Bond will die
For assuredly he is very ill

He went to Church in a May morning
Attended by Fairies one two & three
But the Angels of Providence drove them away
And he returnd home in Misery

He went not out to the Field nor Fold
He went not out to the Village nor Town
But he came home in a black black cloud
And took to his Bed & there lay down

And an Angel of Providence at his Feet
And an Angel of Providence at his Head
And in the midst a Black Black Cloud
And in the midst the Sick Man on his Bed

And on his Right hand was Mary Green
And on his Left hand was his Sister Jane
And their tears fell thro the black black Cloud
To drive away the sick mans pain

O William if thou dost another Love
Dost another Love better than poor Mary
Go & take that other to be thy Wife
And Mary Green shall her Servant be

Yes Mary I do another Love
Another I Love far better than thee
And Another I will have for my Wife
Then what have I to do with thee

For thou art Melancholy Pale
And on thy Head is the cold Moons shine
But she is ruddy & bright as day
And the sun beams dazzle from her eyne

Mary trembled & Mary childd
And Mary fell down on the right hand floor
That William Bond & his Sister Jane
Scarce could recover Mary more

When Mary woke & found her Laid
On the Right hand of her William dear
On the Right hand of his loved Bed
And saw her William Bond so near

The Fairies that fled from William Bond
Danced around her Shining Head
They danced over the Pillow white
And the Angels of Providence left the Bed

I thought Love livd in the hot sun Shine
But O he lives in the Moony light
I thought to find Love in the heat of day
But sweet Love is the Comforter of Night

Seek Love in the Pity of others Woe
In the gentle relief of anothers care
In the darkness of night & the winters snow
In the naked & outcast Seek Love There

"When old corruption first begun"

1   When old corruption first begun
    Adornd in yellow vest
    He committed on flesh a whoredom
    O what a wicked beast

2   From them a callow babe did spring
    And old corruption smild
    To think his race should never end
    For now he had a child

3   He calld him Surgery & fed
    The babe with his own milk
    For flesh & he could neer agree
    She would not let him suck

4   And this he always kept in mind
    And formd a crooked knife
    And ran about with bloody hands
    To seek his mothers life

5   And as he ran to seek his mother
    He met with a dead woman
    He fell in love & married her
    A deed which is not common

6   She soon grew pregnant & brought forth
    Scurvy & spotted fever
    The father grind & skipt about
    And said I'm made for ever

7   For now I have procurd these imps
    Ill try experiments
    With that he tied poor scurvy down
    & stopt up all its vents

8   And when the child began to swell
    He shouted out aloud
    Ive found the dropsy out & soon
    Shall do the world more good

9   He took up fever by the neck
    And cut out all its spots
    And thro the holes which he had made
    He first discoverd guts

"Hail Matrimony made of Love"

Hail Matrimony made of Love
To thy wide gates how great a drove
On purpose to be yok'd do come
Widows & maids & Youths also
That lightly trip on beauty's toe
Or sit on beauty's bum

Hail fingerfooted lovely Creatures
The females of our human Natures
Formed to suckle all Mankind
Tis you that come in time of need
Without you we shoud never Breed
Or any Comfort find

For if a Damsel's blind or lame
Or Nature's hand has crooked her frame
Or if she's deaf or is wall eyed
Yet if her heart is well inclined
Some tender lover she shall find
That panteth for a Bride

The universal Poultice this
To cure whatever is amiss
In damsel or in Widow gay
It makes them smile it makes them skip
Like Birds just cured of the pip
They chirp & hop away

Then come ye Maidens come ye Swains
Come & be eased of all your pains
In Matrimony's Golden cage —

"To Be or Not to Be"

To be or not to be
Of great capacity
Like Sir Isaac Newton
Or Locke or Doctor South
Or Sherlock upon death
Id rather be Sutton

For he did build a house
For aged men & youth
With walls of brick & stone
He furnishd it within
With whatever he could win
And all his own

He drew out of the Stocks
His money in a box
And sent his servant
To Green the Bricklayer
And to the Carpenter
He was so fervent

The chimneys were three score
The windows many more
And for convenience
He sinks & gutters made
And all the way he pavd
To hinder pestilence

Was not this a good man
Whose life was but a span
Whose name was Sutton
As Locke or Doctor South
Or Sherlock upon Death
Or Sir Isaac Newton

"This city & this country has brought forth many mayors"

This city & this country has brought forth many mayors
To sit in state & give forth laws out of their old oak chairs
With face as brown as any nut with drinking of strong ale
Good English hospitality O then it did not fail

With scarlet gowns & broad gold lace would make a yeoman sweat
With stockings rolld above their knees & shoes as black as jet
With eating beef & drinking beer O they were stout & hale
Good English hospitality O then it did not fail

Thus sitting at the table wide the Mayor & Aldermen
Were fit to give law to the city each eat as much as ten
The hungry poor enterd the hall to eat good beef & ale
Good English hospitality O then it did not fail

"Upon a holy thursday their innocent faces clean"

Upon a holy thursday their innocent faces clean
The children walking two & two in grey & blue & green
Grey headed beadles walkd before with wands as white as snow
Till into the high dome of Pauls they like thames waters flow

O what a multitude they seemd, these flowers of London town
Seated in companies they sit with radiance all their own
The hum of multitudes were there but multitudes of lambs
Thousands of little girls & boys raising their innocent hands

Then like a mighty wind they raise to heavn the voice of song
Or like harmonious thunderings the seats of heavn among
Beneath them sit the revrend men the guardians of the poor
Then cherish pity lest you drive an angel from your door

"When the tongues of children are heard on the green"

When the tongues of children are heard on the green
And laughing is heard on the hill
My heart is at rest within my breast
And every thing else is still

Then come home my children the sun is gone down
And the dews of night arise
Come Come leave off play & let us away
Till the morning appears in the skies

No No let us play for it is yet day
And we cannot go to sleep
Besides in the Sky the little birds fly
And the meadows are coverd with Sheep

Well Well go & play till the light fades away
And then go home to bed
The little ones leaped & shouted & laughd
And all the hills ecchoed

"O father father where are you going"

O father father where are you going
O do not walk so fast

O speak father speak to your little boy
Or else I shall be lost

The night it was dark & no father was there
And the child was wet with dew
The mire was deep & the child did weep
And away the vapour flew

"O I say you Joe"

O I say you Joe
Throw us the ball
Ive a good mind to go
And leave you all

I never saw saw such a bowler
To bowl the ball in a tansey
And to clean it with my handkercher
Without saying a word

That Bills a foolish fellow
He has given me a black eye
He does not know how to handle a bat
Any more than a dog or a cat
He has knockd down the wicket
And broke the stumps
And runs without shoes to save his pumps

"Theres Doctor Clash"

Theres Doctor Clash
And Signior Falalasole
O they sweep in the cash
Into their purse hole
Fa me la sol   La me fa Sol

Great A little A
Bouncing B
Play away   Play away
Your out of the key
Fa me la sol   La me fa sol

Musicians should have
A pair of very good ears
And Long fingers & thumbs

And not like clumsy bears
Fa me la sol   La me fa sol

Gentlemen Gentlemen
Rap Rap Rap
Fiddle Fiddle Fiddle
Clap Clap Clap
Fa me la sol   La me fa sol

The Book of Thel

THEL'S MOTTO

Does the Eagle know what is in the pit?
Or wilt thou go ask the Mole:
Can Wisdom be put in a silver rod?
Or Love in a golden bowl?

THEL

I

The daughters of Mne Seraphim led round their sunny flocks.
All but the youngest; she in paleness sought the secret air.
To fade away like morning beauty from her mortal day:
Down by the river of Adona her soft voice is heard:
And thus her gentle lamentation falls like morning dew.

O life of this our spring! why fades the lotus of the water?
Why fade these children of the spring? born but to smile & fall.
Ah! Thel is like a watry bow, and like a parting cloud.
Like a reflection in a glass. like shadows in the water.
Like dreams of infants. like a smile upon an infants face,
Like the doves voice, like transient day, like music in the air;
Ah! gentle may I lay me down, and gentle rest my head.
And gentle sleep the sleep of death. and gentle hear the voice
Of him that walketh in the garden in the evening time.

The Lilly of the valley breathing in the humble grass
Answer'd the lovely maid and said; I am a watry weed,
And I am very small, and love to dwell in lowly vales;
So weak, the gilded butterfly scarce perches on my head.
Yet I am visited from heaven and he that smiles on all.
Walks in the valley. and each morn over me spreads his hand

Saying, rejoice thou humble grass, thou new-born lilly flower,
Thou gentle maid of silent valleys. and of modest brooks;
For thou shalt be clothed in light, and fed with morning manna:
Till summers heat melts thee beside the fountains and the springs
To flourish in eternal vales: then why should Thel complain,
Why should the mistress of the vales of Har, utter a sigh.

She ceasd & smild in tears, then sat down in her silver shrine.

Thel answerd. O thou little virgin of the peaceful valley.
Giving to those that cannot crave, the voiceless, the o'ertired.
Thy breath doth nourish the innocent lamb, he smells thy milky
      garments,
He crops thy flowers. while thou sittest smiling in his face,
Wiping his mild and meekin mouth from all contagious taints.
Thy wine doth purify the golden honey, thy perfume,
Which thou dost scatter on every little blade of grass that springs
Revives the milked cow, & tames the fire-breathing steed.
But Thel is like a faint cloud kindled at the rising sun:
I vanish from my pearly throne, and who shall find my place.

Queen of the vales the Lilly answerd, ask the tender cloud,
And it shall tell thee why it glitters in the morning sky,
And why it scatters its bright beauty thro' the humid air.
Descend O little cloud & hover before the eyes of Thel.

The Cloud descended, and the Lilly bowd her modest head:
And went to mind her numerous charge among the verdant grass.

II

O little Cloud the virgin said, I charge thee tell to me,
Why thou complainest not when in one hour thou fade away:
Then we shall seek thee but not find; ah Thel is like to thee.
I pass away. yet I complain, and no one hears my voice.

The Cloud then shew'd his golden head & his bright form emerg'd,
Hovering and glittering on the air before the face of Thel.

O virgin know'st thou not. our steeds drink of the golden springs
Where Luvah doth renew his horses: look'st thou on my youth,
And fearest thou because I vanish and am seen no more.
Nothing remains; O maid I tell thee, when I pass away,
It is to tenfold life, to love, to peace, and raptures holy:
Unseen descending, weigh my light wings upon balmy flowers;
And court the fair eyed dew. to take me to her shining tent;
The weeping virgin, trembling kneels before the risen sun,

Till we arise link'd in a golden band, and never part;
But walk united, bearing food to all our tender flowers

Dost thou O little Cloud? I fear that I am not like thee;
For I walk through the vales of Har. and smell the sweetest flowers;
But I feed not the little flowers: I hear the warbling birds,
But I feed not the warbling birds. they fly and seek their food;
But Thel delights in these no more because I fade away,
And all shall say, without a use this shining woman liv'd,
Or did she only live. to be at death the food of worms.

The Cloud reclind upon his airy throne and answer'd thus.

Then if thou art the food of worms. O virgin of the skies,
How great thy use. how great thy blessing; every thing that lives,
Lives not alone, nor for itself: fear not and I will call
The weak worm from its lowly bed, and thou shalt hear its voice.
Come forth worm of the silent valley, to thy pensive queen.

The helpless worm arose, and sat upon the Lillys leaf,
And the bright Cloud saild on, to find his partner in the vale.

III
Then Thel astonish'd view'd the Worm upon its dewy bed.

Art thou a Worm? image of weakness. art thou but a Worm?
I see thee like an infant wrapped in the Lillys leaf:
Ah weep not little voice, thou can'st not speak. but thou can'st
     weep;
Is this a Worm? I see thee lay helpless & naked: weeping,
And none to answer, none to cherish thee with mothers smiles.

The Clod of Clay heard the Worms voice, & raisd her pitying head;
She bow'd over the weeping infant, and her life exhal'd
In milky fondness, then on Thel she fix'd her humble eyes.

O beauty of the vales of Har. we live not for ourselves,
Thou seest me the meanest thing, and so I am indeed;
My bosom of itself is cold. and of itself is dark,
But he that loves the lowly, pours his oil upon my head.
And kisses me, and binds his nuptial bands around my breast.
And says; Thou mother of my children, I have loved thee.
And I have given thee a crown that none can take away
But how this is sweet maid, I know not, and I cannot know,

I ponder, and I cannot ponder; yet I live and love.

The daughter of beauty wip'd her pitying tears with her white veil,
And said. Alas! I knew not this, and therefore did I weep:
That God would love a Worm I knew, and punish the evil foot
That wilful, bruis'd its helpless form: but that he cherish'd it
With milk and oil, I never knew; and therefore did I weep,
And I complaind in the mild air, because I fade away,
And lay me down in thy cold bed, and leave my shining lot.
Queen of the vales, the matron Clay answerd; I heard thy sighs.
And all thy moans flew o'er my roof. but I have call'd them down:
Wilt thou O Queen enter my house. 'tis given thee to enter,
And to return; fear nothing. enter with thy virgin feet.

IV

The eternal gates terrific porter lifted the northern bar:
Thel enter'd in & saw the secrets of the land unknown;
She saw the couches of the dead, & where the fibrous roots
Of every heart on earth infixes deep its restless twists:
A land of sorrows & of tears where never smile was seen.

She wanderd in the land of clouds thro' valleys dark, listning
Dolours & lamentations: waiting oft beside a dewy grave
She stood in silence. listning to the voices of the ground,
Till to her own grave plot she came, & there she sat down.
And heard this voice of sorrow breathed from the hollow pit.

Why cannot the Ear be closed to its own destruction?
Or the glistning Eye to the poison of a smile!
Why are Eyelids stord with arrows ready drawn,
Where a thousand fighting men in ambush lie?
Or an Eye of gifts & graces, show'ring fruits & coined gold!
Why a Tongue impress'd with honey from every wind?
Why an Ear, a whirlpool fierce to draw creations in?
Why a Nostril wide inhaling terror trembling & affright.
Why a tender curb upon the youthful burning boy!
Why a little curtain of flesh on the bed of our desire?

The Virgin started from her seat, & with a shriek.
Fled back unhinderd till she came into the vales of Har

A Divine Image

[AN EARLY SONG OF EXPERIENCE INCLUDED IN ONE LATE
    COPY]

Cruelty has a Human Heart
And Jealousy a Human Face
Terror, the Human Form Divine
And Secrecy, the Human Dress

The Human Dress, is forged Iron
The Human Form, a fiery Forge.
The Human Face, a Furnace seal'd
The Human Heart, its hungry Gorge.

Motto to the Songs of Innocence & of Experience

The Good are attracted by Mens perceptions
    And Think not for themselves
    Till Experience teaches them to catch
    And to cage the Fairies & Elves

And then the Knave begins to snarl
And the Hypocrite to howl
And all his good Friends shew their private ends
And the Eagle is known from the Owl

"Let the Brothels of Paris be opened"

Let the Brothels of Paris be opened
With many an alluring dance
To awake the Physicians thro the city
Said the beautiful Queen of France

Then old Nobodaddy aloft
Farted & belchd & coughd
And said I love hanging & drawing & quartering
Every bit as well as war & slaughtering

Then he swore a great & solemn Oath
To kill the people I am loth
But If they rebel they must go to hell
They shall have a Priest & a passing bell

The King awoke on his couch of gold
As soon as he heard these tidings told
Arise & come both fife & drum
And the [*Famine*]* shall eat both crust & crumb

The Queen of France just touchd this Globe
And the Pestilence darted from her robe
But our good Queen quite grows to the ground
And a great many suckers grow all around

"Who will exchange his own fire side"

Who will exchange his own fire side
For the stone of anothers door
Who will exchange his wheaten loaf
For the links of a dungeon floor

Fayette beheld the King & Queen
In curses & iron bound
But mute Fayette wept tear for tear
And guarded them around

O who would smile on the wintry seas
& Pity the stormy roar
Or who will exchange his new born child
For the dog at the wintry door

"When Klopstock England defied"

When Klopstock England defied
Uprose terrible Blake in his pride
For old Nobodaddy aloft
Farted & Belchd & coughd
Then swore a great oath that made heavn quake
And calld aloud to English Blake
Blake was giving his body ease
At Lambeth beneath the poplar trees
From his seat then started he
And turnd himself round three times three
The Moon at that sight blushd scarlet red
The stars threw down their cups & fled

---

* The word "Famine" was deleted but not replaced by Blake.

And all the devils that were in hell
Answered with a ninefold yell
Klopstock felt the intripled turn
And all his bowels began to churn
And his bowels turned round three times three
And lockd in his soul with a ninefold key
That from his body it neer could be parted
Till to the last trumpet it was farted
Then again old nobodaddy swore
He neer had seen such a thing before
Since Noah was shut in the ark
Since Eve first chose her hell fire spark
Since twas the fashion to go naked
Since the old anything was created
And in pity he begd him to turn again
And ease poor Klopstocks nine fold pain
From pity then he redend round
And the ninefold Spell unwound
If Blake could do this when he rose up from shite
What might he not do if he sat down to write

"Great things are done when men & mountains meet"

Great things are done when Men & Mountains meet
This is not Done by Jostling in the Street

"If you play a Game of Chance know before you begin"

If you play a Game of Chance know before you begin
If you are benevolent you will never win

"If I eer Grow to Mans Estate"

If I eer Grow to Mans Estate
O Give to me a Womans fate
May I govern all both great & small
Have the last word & take the wall

The Argument

[FROM *THE MARRIAGE OF HEAVEN AND HELL*]

Rintrah roars & shakes his fires in the burdend air;
Hungry clouds swag on the deep

Once meek, and in a perilous path,
The just man kept his course along
The vale of death.
Roses are planted where thorns grow.
And on the barren heath
Sing the honey bees.

Then the perilous path was planted:
And a river, and a spring
On every cliff and tomb;
And on the bleached bones
Red clay brought forth.

Till the villain left the paths of ease,
To walk in perilous paths, and drive
The just man into barren climes.

Now the sneaking serpent walks
In mild humility.
And the just man rages in the wilds
Where lions roam.

Rintrah roars & shakes his fires in the burdend air;
Hungry clouds swag on the deep.

Proverbs of Hell

In seed time learn, in harvest teach, in winter enjoy.

Drive your cart and your plow over the bones of the dead.
The road of excess leads to the palace of wisdom.

Prudence is a rich ugly old maid courted by Incapacity.
He who desires but acts not, breeds pestilence.

The cut worm forgives the plow.

Dip him in the river who loves water.

A fool sees not the same tree that a wise man sees.
He whose face gives no light, shall never become a star.
Eternity is in love with the productions of time.
The busy bee has no time for sorrow.
The hours of folly are measur'd by the clock, but of wisdom: no
    clock can measure.

All wholsom food is caught without a net or a trap.
Bring out number weight & measure in a year of dearth.

No bird soars too high. if he soars with his own wings.

A dead body. revenges not injuries.

The most sublime act is to set another before you.

If the fool would persist in his folly he would become wise
Folly is the cloke of knavery.

Shame is Prides cloke.

Prisons are built with stones of Law, Brothels with bricks of Reli-
    gion.
The pride of the peacock is the glory of God.
The lust of the goat is the bounty of God.
The wrath of the lion is the wisdom of God.
The nakedness of woman is the work of God.

Excess of sorrow laughs. Excess of joy weeps.

The roaring of lions, the howling of wolves, the raging of the stormy
    sea, and the destructive sword. are portions of eternity too
    great for the eye of man.

The fox condemns the trap, not himself.

Joys impregnate. Sorrows bring forth.

Let man wear the fell of the lion. woman the fleece of the sheep.

The bird a nest, the spider a web, man friendship.

The selfish smiling fool. & the sullen frowning fool. shall be both
    thought wise. that they may be a rod.

What is now proved was once, only imagin'd.
The rat, the mouse, the fox, the rabbet; watch the roots, the lion,
    the tyger, the horse, the elephant, watch the fruits.

The cistern contains: the fountain overflows

One thought. fills immensity.
Always be ready to speak your mind, and a base man will avoid you.

Every thing possible to be believ'd is an image of truth.

The eagle never lost so much time. as when he submitted to learn
    of the crow.

The fox provides for himself. but God provides for the lion.
Think in the morning, Act in the noon, Eat in the evening, Sleep
    in the night.
He who has sufferd you to impose on him knows you.
As the plow follows words, so God rewards prayers.

The tygers of wrath are wiser than the horses of instruction

Expect poison from the standing water.

You never know what is enough unless you know what is more than
    enough.

Listen to the fools reproach! it is a kingly title!

The eyes of fire, the nostrils of air, the mouth of water, the beard of
    earth.

The weak in courage is strong in cunning.
The apple tree never asks the beech how he shall grow, nor the
    lion. the horse; how he shall take his prey.
The thankful reciever bears a plentiful harvest.

If others had not been foolish. we should be so.
The soul of sweet delight. can never be defil'd,

When thou seest an Eagle, thou seest a portion of Genius. lift up
    thy head!
As the catterpiller chooses the fairest leaves to lay her eggs on, so
    the priest lays his curse on the fairest joys.

To create a little flower is the labour of ages.

Damn. braces: Bless relaxes.

The best wine is the oldest. the best water the newest.
Prayers plow not! Praises reap not!
Joys laugh not! Sorrows weep not!

The head Sublime, the heart Pathos, the genitals Beauty, the hands
    & feet Proportion.

As the air to a bird or the sea to a fish, so is contempt to the contemptible.

The crow wish'd every thing was black, the owl, that every thing was white.

Exuberance is Beauty.

If the lion was advised by the fox. he would be cunning.

Improvement makes strait roads, but the crooked roads without Improvement, are roads of Genius.

Sooner murder an infant in its cradle than nurse unacted desires

Where man is not nature is barren.

Truth can never be told so as to be understood, and not be believ'd.

Enough! or Too much

A Song of Liberty

1. The Eternal Female groand! it was heard over all the Earth:
2. Albions coast is sick silent; the American meadows faint!
3. Shadows of Prophecy shiver along by the lakes and the rivers and mutter across the ocean! France rend down thy dungeon;
4. Golden Spain burst the barriers of old Rome;
5. Cast thy keys O Rome into the deep down falling, even to eternity down falling,
6. And weep!
7. In her trembling hands she took the new born terror howling;
8. On those infinite mountains of light now barr'd out by the atlantic sea, the new born fire stood before the starry king!
9. Flag'd with grey brow'd snows and thunderous visages the jealous wings wav'd over the deep.
10. The speary hand burned aloft, unbuckled was the shield, forth went the hand of jealousy among the flaming hair, and hurl'd the new born wonder thro' the starry night.
11. The fire, the fire, is falling!
12. Look up! look up! O citizen of London. enlarge thy countenance; O Jew, leave counting gold! return to thy oil and wine; O African! black African! (go. winged thought widen his forehead.)
13. The fiery limbs, the flaming hair, shot like the sinking sun into the western sea.

14. Wak'd from his eternal sleep, the hoary element roaring fled away:
15. Down rushd beating his wings in vain the jealous king: his grey brow'd councellors, thunderous warriors, curl'd veterans, among helms, and shields, and chariots horses, elephants: banners, castles, slings and rocks,
16. Falling, rushing, ruining! buried in the ruins, on Urthona's dens.
17. All night beneath the ruins, then their sullen flames faded emerge round the gloomy king,
18. With thunder and fire: leading his starry hosts thro' the waste wilderness he promulgates his ten commands, glancing his beamy eyelids over the deep in dark dismay,
19. Where the son of fire in his eastern cloud, while the morning plumes her golden breast,
20. Spurning the clouds written with curses, stamps the stony law to dust, loosing the eternal horses from the dens of night; crying

Empire is no more! and now the lion & wolf shall cease.

Preludium

[FROM *AMERICA A PROPHECY*]

The shadowy daughter of Urthona stood before red Orc.
When fourteen suns had faintly journey'd o'er his dark abode;
His food she brought in iron baskets, his drink in cups of iron;
Crown'd with a helmet & dark hair the nameless female stood;
A quiver with its burning stores, a bow like that of night,
When pestilence is shot from heaven; no other arms she need:
Invulnerable tho' naked, save where clouds roll round her loins,
Their awful folds in the dark air; silent she stood as night;
For never from her iron tongue could voice or sound arise;
But dumb till that dread day when Orc assay'd his fierce embrace.

Dark virgin; said the hairy youth, thy father stern abhorr'd;
Rivets my tenfold chains while still on high my spirit soars;
Sometimes an eagle screaming in the sky, sometimes a lion,
Stalking upon the mountains, & sometimes a whale I lash

The raging fathomless abyss, anon a serpent folding
Around the pillars of Urthona, and round thy dark limbs,
On the Canadian wilds I fold, feeble my spirit folds.
For chaind beneath I rend these caverns; when thou bringest food
I howl my joy! and my red eyes seek to behold thy face
In vain! these clouds roll to & fro, & hide thee from my sight.

Silent as despairing love, and strong as jealousy,
The hairy shoulders rend the links, free are the wrists of fire;
Round the terrific loins he siez'd the panting struggling womb;
It joy'd: she put aside her clouds & smiled her first-born smile;
As when a black cloud shews its light'nings to the silent deep.

Soon as she saw the terrible boy then burst the virgin cry.

I know thee, I have found thee, & I will not let thee go;
Thou art the image of God who dwells in darkness of Africa;
And thou art fall'n to give me life in regions of dark death.
On my American plains I feel the struggling afflictions
Endur'd by roots that writhe their arms into the nether deep:
I see a serpent in Canada, who courts me to his love;
In Mexico an Eagle, and a Lion in Peru;
I see a Whale in the South-sea, drinking my soul away.
O what limb rending pains I feel. thy fire & my frost
Mingle in howling pains, in furrows by thy lightnings rent;
This is eternal death; and this the torment long foretold.

The Song of Los

AFRICA

I will sing you a song of Los. the Eternal Prophet:
He sung it to four harps at the tables of Eternity.
          In heart-formed Africa.
Urizen faded! Ariston shudderd!
      And thus the Song began

Adam stood in the garden of Eden:
And Noah on the mountains of Ararat;
They saw Urizen give his Laws to the Nations
By the hands of the children of Los.

Adam shudderd! Noah faded! black grew the sunny African
When Rintrah gave Abstract Philosophy to Brama in the East:

(Night spoke to the Cloud!
Lo these Human form'd spirits in smiling hipocrisy. War
Against one another; so let them War on; slaves to the eternal
    Elements)
Noah shrunk, beneath the waters;
Abram fled in fires from Chaldea;
Moses beheld upon Mount Sinai forms of dark delusion:

To Trismegistus. Palamabron gave an abstract Law:
To Pythagoras Socrates & Plato.

Times rolled on o'er all the sons of Har, time after time
Orc on Mount Atlas howld, chain'd down with the Chain of
    Jealousy
Then Oothoon hoverd over Judah & Jerusalem
And Jesus heard her voice (a man of sorrows) he recievd
A Gospel from wretched Theotormon.

The human race began to wither, for the healthy built
Secluded places, fearing the joys of Love
And the disease'd only propagated:
So Antamon call'd up Leutha from her valleys of delight:
And to Mahomet a loose Bible gave.
But in the North, to Odin, Sotha gave a Code of War,
Because of Diralada thinking to reclaim his joy.

These were the Churches: Hospitals: Castles: Palaces:
Like nets & gins & traps to catch the joys of Eternity
    And all the rest a desart;
Till like a dream Eternity was obliterated & erased.

Since that dread day when Har and Heva fled.
Because their brethren & sisters liv'd in War & Lust;
And as they fled they shrunk
Into two narrow doleful forms:
Creeping in reptile flesh upon
The bosom of the ground:
And all the vast of Nature shrunk
Before their shrunken eyes.

Thus the terrible race of Los & Enitharmon gave
Laws & Religions to the sons of Har binding them more

And more to Earth: closing and restraining:
Till a Philosophy of Five Senses was complete
Urizen wept & gave it into the hands of Newton & Locke

Clouds roll heavy upon the Alps round Rousseau & Voltaire:
And on the mountains of Lebanon round the deceased Gods
Of Asia; & on the desarts of Africa round the Fallen Angels
The Guardian Prince of Albion burns in his nightly tent

ASIA

The Kings of Asia heard
The howl rise up from Europe!
And each ran out from his Web;
From his ancient woven Den;
For the darkness of Asia was startled
At the thick-flaming, thought-creating fires of Orc.

And the Kings of Asia stood
And cried in bitterness of soul.

Shall not the King call for Famine from the heath?
Nor the Priest, for Pestilence from the fen?
To restrain! to dismay! to thin!
The inhabitants of mountain and plain;
In the day, of full-feeding prosperity;
And the night of delicious songs.

Shall not the Councellor throw his curb
Of Poverty on the laborious?
To fix the price of labour;
To invent allegoric riches:

And the privy admonishers of men
Call for fires in the City
For heaps of smoking ruins,
In the night of prosperity & wantonness
To turn man from his path,
To restrain the child from the womb,
To cut off the bread from the city,
That the remnant may learn to obey.

That the pride of the heart may fail;
That the lust of the eyes may be quench'd:
That the delicate ear in its infancy

May be dull'd; and the nostrils clos'd up;
To teach mortal worms the path
That leads from the gates of the Grave.

Urizen heard them cry!
And his shudd'ring waving wings
Went enormous above the red flames
Drawing clouds of despair thro' the heavens
Of Europe as he went:
And his Books of brass iron & gold
Melted over the land as he flew,
Heavy-waving, howling, weeping.

And he stood over Judea:
And stay'd in his ancient place:
And stretch'd his clouds over Jerusalem;

For Adam, a mouldering skeleton
Lay bleach'd on the garden of Eden;
And Noah as white as snow
On the mountains of Ararat.

Then the thunders of Urizen bellow'd aloud
From his woven darkness above.

Orc raging in European darkness
Arose like a pillar of fire above the Alps
Like a serpent of fiery flame!
  The sullen Earth
  Shrunk!

Forth from the dead dust rattling bones to bones
Join: shaking convuls'd the shivring clay breathes
And all flesh naked stands: Fathers and Friends;
Mothers & Infants; Kings & Warriors:

The Grave shrieks with delight, & shakes
Her hollow womb, & clasps the solid stem:
Her bosom swells with wild desire:
And milk & blood & glandous wine
In rivers rush & shout & dance,
On mountain, dale and plain.

   The SONG of LOS is Ended.
    Urizen Wept.

"And did those feet in ancient time"*

[FROM MILTON]

And did those feet in ancient time,
Walk upon Englands mountains green:
And was the holy Lamb of God,
On Englands pleasant pastures seen!

And did the Countenance Divine,
Shine forth upon our clouded hills?
And was Jerusalem builded here,
Among these dark Satanic Mills?

Bring me my Bow of burning gold:
Bring me my Arrows of desire:
Bring me my Spear: O clouds unfold!
Bring me my Chariot of fire!

I will not cease from Mental Fight,
Nor shall my Sword sleep in my hand:
Till we have built Jerusalem,
In Englands green & pleasant Land.

"The fields from Islington to Marybone"

The fields from Islington to Marybone,
To Primrose Hill and Saint Johns Wood:
    Were builded over with pillars of gold,
And there Jerusalems pillars stood.

    Her Little-ones ran on the fields
The Lamb of God among them seen
    And fair Jerusalem his Bride:
Among the little meadows green.

    Pancrass & Kentish-town repose
Among her golden pillars high:
    Among her golden arches which
Shine upon the starry sky.

---

* This poem, out of its context and retitled *Jerusalem*, is famous as a hymn, the
  music composed by Charles Hubert Hastings Parry (1848–1918).

The Jews-harp-house & the Green Man;
The Ponds where Boys to bathe delight:
The fields of Cows by Willans farm:
Shine in Jerusalems pleasant sight.

She walks upon our meadows green:
The Lamb of God walks by her side:
And every English Child is seen,
Children of Jesus & his Bride,

Forgiving trespasses and sins
Lest Babylon with cruel Og,
With Moral & Self-righteous Law
Should Crucify in Satans Synagogue!

What are those golden Builders doing
Near mournful ever-weeping Paddington
Standing above that mighty Ruin
Where Satan the first victory won.

Where Albion slept beneath the Fatal Tree
And the Druids golden Knife,
Rioted in human gore,
In Offerings of Human Life

They groan'd aloud on London Stone
They groan'd aloud on Tyburns Brook
Albion gave his deadly groan,
And all the Atlantic Mountains shook

Albions Spectre from his Loins
Tore forth in all the pomp of War!
Satan his name: in flames of fire
He stretch'd his Druid Pillars far.

Jerusalem fell from Lambeth's Vale,
Down thro Poplar & Old Bow;
Thro Malden & acros the Sea,
In War & howling death & woe.

The Rhine was red with human blood:
The Danube rolld a purple tide:
On the Euphrates Satan stood:
And over Asia stretch'd his pride.

He witherd up sweet Zions Hill,
From every Nation of the Earth:

He witherd up Jerusalems Gates,
And in a dark Land gave her birth.

He witherd up the Human Form,
By laws of sacrifice for sin:
Till it became a Mortal Worm:
But O! translucent all within.

The Divine Vision still was seen
Still was the Human Form, Divine
Weeping in weak & mortal clay
O Jesus still the Form was thine.

And thine the Human Face & thine
The Human Hands & Feet & Breath
Entering thro' the Gates of Birth
And passing thro' the Gates of Death

And O thou Lamb of God, whom I
Slew in my dark self-righteous pride:
Art thou return'd to Albions Land!
And is Jerusalem thy Bride?

Come to my arms & never more
Depart; but dwell for ever here:
Create my Spirit to thy Love:
Subdue my Spectre to thy Fear.

Spectre of Albion! warlike Fiend!
In clouds of blood & ruin roll'd:
I here reclaim thee as my own
My Selfhood! Satan! armd in gold.

Is this thy soft Family-Love
Thy cruel Patriarchal pride
Planting thy Family alone
Destroying all the World beside.

A mans worst enemies are those
Of his own house & family;
And he who makes his law a curse,
By his own law shall surely die.

In my Exchanges every Land
Shall walk, & mine in every Land,
Mutual shall build Jerusalem:
Both heart in heart & hand in hand.

"I saw a Monk of Charlemaine"

I saw a Monk of Charlemaine
Arise before my sight
    I talkd with the Grey Monk as we stood
In beams of infernal light

    Gibbon arose with a lash of steel
And Voltaire with a wracking wheel
    The Schools in clouds of learning rolld
Arose with War in iron & gold.

    Thou lazy Monk they sound afar
In vain condemning glorious War
    And in your Cell you shall ever dwell
Rise War & bind him in his Cell.

    The blood. red ran from the Grey Monks side
His hands & feet were wounded wide
    His body bent, his arms & knees
Like to the roots of ancient trees

    When Satan first the black bow bent
And the Moral Law from the Gospel rent
    He forgd the Law into a Sword
And spilld the blood of mercys Lord.

    Titus! Constantine! Charlemaine!
O Voltaire! Rousseau! Gibbon! Vain
    Your Grecian Mocks & Roman Sword
Against this image of his Lord!

    For a Tear is an Intellectual thing;
And a Sigh is the Sword of an Angel King
    And the bitter groan of a Martyrs woe
Is an Arrow from the Almighties Bow!

[From *The Everlasting Gospel*]

[PREFACE]

I will tell you what Joseph of Arimathea
Said to my Fairy was not it very queer
Pliny & Trajan what are You here
Come listen to Joseph of Arimathea
Listen patient & when Joseph has done
Twill make a fool laugh & a Fairy Fun

What can be done with such desperate Fools
Who follow after the Heathen Schools
I was standing by when Jesus died
What I calld Humility they calld Pride

THE EVERLASTING GOSPEL

Was Jesus Humble or did he
Give any Proofs of Humility
Boast of high Things with Humble tone
And give with Charity a Stone
When but a Child he ran away
And left his Parents in Dismay
When they had wanderd three days long
These were the words upon his tongue
No Earthly Parents I confess
I am doing my Fathers business
When the rich learned Pharisee
Came to consult him secretly
Upon his heart with Iron pen
He wrote Ye must be born again
He was too proud to take a bribe
He spoke with authority not like a Scribe
He says with most consummate Art
Follow me I am meek & lowly of heart
As that is the only way to escape
The Misers net & the Gluttons trap
He who loves his Enemies betrays his Friends
This surely is not what Jesus intends

But the sneaking Pride of Heroic Schools
And the Scribes & Pharisees Virtuous Rules
For he acts with honest triumphant Pride
And this is the cause that Jesus died
He did not die with Christian Ease
Asking Pardon of his Enemies
If he had Caiphas would forgive
Sneaking submission can always live
He had only to say that God was the devil
And the devil was God like a Christian Civil
Mild Christian regrets to the devil confess
For affronting him thrice in the Wilderness
He had soon been bloody Caesars Elf
And at last he would have been Caesar himself
Like d^r Priestly & Bacon & Newton
Poor Spiritual Knowledge is not worth a button
For thus the Gospel Sr Isaac confutes
God can only be known by his Attributes
And as for the Indwelling of the Holy Ghost
Or of Christ & his Father its all a boast
And Pride & Vanity of Imagination
That disdains to follow this Worlds Fashion
To teach doubt & Experiment
Certainly was not what Christ meant
What was he doing all that time
From twelve years old to manly prime
Was he then Idle or the Less
About his Fathers business
Or was his wisdom held in scorn
Before his wrath began to burn
In Miracles throughout the Land
That quite unnervd Lord Caiaphas hand
If he had been Antichrist Creeping Jesus
Hed have done any thing to please us
Gone sneaking into Synagogues
And not usd the Elders & Priests like dogs
But Humble as a Lamb or Ass
Obeyd himself to Caiaphas
God wants not Man to Humble himself
This is the trick of the ancient Elf
This is the Race that Jesus ran
Humble to God Haughty to Man

Cursing the Rulers before the People
Even to the temples highest Steeple
And when he Humbled himself to God
Then descended the Cruel Rod
If thou humblest thyself thou humblest me
Thou also dwellst in Eternity
Thou art a Man God is no more
Thy own humanity learn to adore
For that is my Spirit of Life
Awake arise to Spiritual Strife
And thy Revenge abroad display
In terrors at the Last Judgment day
Gods Mercy & Long Suffering
Is but the Sinner to Judgment to bring
Thou on the Cross for them shalt pray
And take Revenge at the Last Day
Jesus replied & thunders hurld
I never will Pray for the World
Once [I] did so when I prayd in the Garden
I wishd to take with me a Bodily Pardon
Can that which was of Woman born
In the absence of the Morn
When the Soul fell into Sleep
And Archangels round it weep
Shooting out against the Light
Fibres of a deadly night
Reasoning upon its own Dark Fiction
In Doubt which is Self Contradiction
Humility is only Doubt
And does the Sun & Moon blot out
Rooting over with thorns & stems
The buried Soul & all its Gems
This Lifes dim Windows of the Soul
Distorts the Heavens from Pole to Pole
And leads you to Believe a Lie
When you see with not thro the Eye
That was born in a night to perish in a night
When the Soul slept in the beams of Light.

Was Jesus Chaste or did he
Give any Lessons of Chastity
The morning blushd fiery red

Mary was found in Adulterous bed
Earth groand beneath & Heaven above
Trembled at discovery of Love
Jesus was sitting in Moses Chair
They brought the trembling Woman There
Moses commands she be stoned to Death
What was the sound of Jesus breath
He laid his hand on Moses Law
The Ancient Heavens in Silent Awe
Writ with Curses from Pole to Pole
All away began to roll
The Earth trembling & Naked lay
In secret bed of Mortal Clay
On Sinai felt the hand Divine
Putting back the bloody shrine
And she heard the breath of God
As she heard by Edens flood
Good & Evil are no more
Sinais trumpets cease to roar
Cease finger of God to Write
The Heavens are not clean in thy Sight
Thou art Good & thou Alone
Nor may the sinner cast one stone
To be Good only is to be
A Devil or else a Pharisee
Thou Angel of the Presence Divine
That didst create this Body of Mine
Wherefore has[t] thou writ these Laws
And Created Hells dark jaws
My Presence I will take from thee
A Cold Leper thou shalt be
Tho thou wast so pure & bright
That Heaven was Impure in thy Sight
Tho thy Oath turnd Heaven Pale
Tho thy Covenant built Hells Jail
Tho thou didst all to Chaos roll
With the Serpent for its soul
Still the breath Divine does move
And the breath Divine is Love
Mary Fear Not Let me see
The Seven Devils that torment thee
Hide not from my Sight thy Sin

That forgiveness thou maist win
Has no Man Condemned thee
No Man Lord! then what is he
Who shall Accuse thee. Come Ye forth
Fallen Fiends of Heavnly birth
That have forgot your Ancient love
And driven away my trembling Dove
You shall bow before her feet
You shall lick the dust for Meat
And tho you cannot Love but Hate
Shall be beggars at Loves Gate
What was thy love Let me see it
Was it love or Dark Deceit
Love too long from Me has fled.
Twas dark deceit to Earn my bread
Twas Covet or twas Custom or
Some trifle not worth caring for
That they may call a shame & Sin
Loves Temple that God dwelleth in
And hide in secret hidden Shrine
The Naked Human form divine
And render that a Lawless thing
On which the Soul Expands its wing
But this O Lord this was my Sin
When first I let these Devils in
In dark pretence to Chastity
Blaspheming Love blaspheming thee
Thence Rose Secret Adulteries
And thence did Covet also rise
My Sin thou hast forgiven me
Canst thou forgive my Blasphemy
Canst thou return to this dark Hell
And in my burning bosom dwell
And canst thou Die that I may live
And canst thou Pity & forgive
Then Rolld the shadowy Man away
From the Limbs of Jesus to make them his prey
An Ever devo[u]ring appetite
Glittering with festering Venoms bright
Crying Crucify this cause of distress
Who dont keep the secrets of Holiness
All Mental Powers by Diseases we bind

But he heals the Deaf & the Dumb & the Blind
Whom God has afflicted for Secret Ends
He comforts & Heals & calls them Friends
But when Jesus was Crucified
Then was perfected his glittring pride
In three Nights he devourd his prey
And still he devours the Body of Clay
For Dust & Clay is the Serpents meat
Which never was made for Man to Eat

Was Jesus gentle or did he
Give any marks of Gentility
When twelve years old he ran away
And left his Parents in dismay
When after three days sorrow found
Loud as Sinai's trumpet sound
No Earthly Parents I confess
My Heavenly Fathers business
Ye understand not what I say
And angry force me to obey
Obedience is a duty then
And favour gains with God & Men
John from the Wilderness loud cried
Satan gloried in his Pride
Come said Satan come away
Ill soon see if youll obey
John for disobedience bled
But you can turn the stones to bread
Gods high king & Gods high Priest
Shall Plant their Glories in your breast
If Caiaphas you will obey
If Herod you with bloody Prey
Feed with the Sacrifice & be
Obedient fall down worship me
Thunders & lightnings broke around
And Jesus voice in thunders sound
Thus I sieze the Spiritual Prey
Ye smiters with disease make way
I come Your King & God to sieze
Is God a Smiter with disease
The God of this World raged in vain
He bound Old Satan in his Chain

And bursting forth his furious ire
Became a Chariot of fire
Throughout the land he took his course
And traced Diseases to their Source
He cursd the Scribe & Pharisee
Trampling down Hipocrisy
Where eer his Chariot took its way
There Gates of Death let in the Day
Broke down from every Chain & Bar
And Satan in his Spiritual War
Dragd at his Chariot wheels loud howld
The God of this World louder rolld
The Chariot Wheels & louder still
His voice was heard from Zions hill
And in his hand the Scourge shone bright
He scourgd the Merchant Canaanite
From out the Temple of his Mind
And in his Body tight does bind
Satan & all his Hellish Crew
And thus with wrath he did subdue
The Serpent Bulk of Natures dross
Till he had naild it to the Cross
He took on Sin in the Virgins Womb
And put it off on the Cross & Tomb
To be Worshipd by the Church of Rome

The Vision of Christ that thou dost see
Is my Visions Greatest Enemy
Thine has a great hook nose like thine
Mine has a snub nose like to mine
Thine is the Friend of All Mankind
Mine speaks in parables to the Blind
Thine loves the same world that mine hates
Thy Heaven doors are my Hell Gates
Socrates taught what Melitus
Loathd as a Nations bitterest Curse
And Caiphas was in his own Mind
A benefactor of Mankind
Both read the Bible day & night
But thou readst black where I read white

Alphabetical List of Titles and First Lines

(Titles indicated in italics)

DOVER · THRIFT · EDITIONS

POETRY

THE CONGO AND OTHER POEMS, Vachel Lindsay. 96pp. 27272-9

EVANGELINE AND OTHER POEMS, Henry Wadsworth Longfellow. 64pp. 28255-4

FAVORITE POEMS, Henry Wadsworth Longfellow. 96pp. 27273-7

"TO HIS COY MISTRESS" AND OTHER POEMS, Andrew Marvell. 64pp. 29544-3

SPOON RIVER ANTHOLOGY, Edgar Lee Masters. 144pp. 27275-3

SELECTED POEMS, Claude McKay. 80pp. 40876-0

RENASCENCE AND OTHER POEMS, Edna St. Vincent Millay. 64pp. (Not available in Europe or the United Kingdom) 26873-X

FIRST FIG AND OTHER POEMS, Edna St. Vincent Millay. 80pp. (Not available in Europe or the United Kingdom) 41104-4

SELECTED POEMS, John Milton. 128pp. 27554-X

CIVIL WAR POETRY: An Anthology, Paul Negri (ed.). 128pp. 29883-3

ENGLISH VICTORIAN POETRY: AN ANTHOLOGY, Paul Negri (ed.). 256pp. 40425-0

GREAT SONNETS, Paul Negri (ed.). 96pp. 28052-7

THE RAVEN AND OTHER FAVORITE POEMS, Edgar Allan Poe. 64pp. 26685-0

ESSAY ON MAN AND OTHER POEMS, Alexander Pope. 128pp. 28053-5

GOBLIN MARKET AND OTHER POEMS, Christina Rossetti. 64pp. 28055-1

CHICAGO POEMS, Carl Sandburg. 80pp. 28057-8

CORNHUSKERS, Carl Sandburg. 157pp. 41409-4

THE SHOOTING OF DAN MCGREW AND OTHER POEMS, Robert Service. 96pp. (Available in U.S. only.) 27556-6

COMPLETE SONNETS, William Shakespeare. 80pp. 26686-9

SELECTED POEMS, Percy Bysshe Shelley. 128pp. 27558-2

AFRICAN-AMERICAN POETRY: An Anthology, 1773–1930, Joan R. Sherman (ed.). 96pp. 29604-0

NATIVE AMERICAN SONGS AND POEMS: An Anthology, Brian Swann (ed.). 64pp. 29450-1

SELECTED POEMS, Alfred Lord Tennyson. 112pp. 27282-6

AENEID, Vergil (Publius Vergilius Maro). 256pp. 28749-1

GREAT LOVE POEMS, Shane Weller (ed.). 128pp. 27284-2

CIVIL WAR POETRY AND PROSE, Walt Whitman. 96pp. 28507-3

SELECTED POEMS, Walt Whitman. 128pp. 26878-0

THE BALLAD OF READING GAOL AND OTHER POEMS, Oscar Wilde. 64pp. 27072-6

EARLY POEMS, William Carlos Williams. 64pp. (Available in U.S. only.) 29294-0

FAVORITE POEMS, William Wordsworth. 80pp. 27073-4

EARLY POEMS, William Butler Yeats. 128pp. 27808-5